IT WILL TAKE A LIFETIME

IT WILL TAKE A LIFETIME

Francis Sweeney

Charles River Books, Inc., Boston

Library of Congress Cataloging in Publication Data

Sweeney, Francis W.   1916-
    It will take a life time.

    I. Title.
    PS3537.W4418   814'.54   80-10986
    ISBN 0-9182-018-3

Published by Charles River Books, Inc.
One Thompson Square, Boston, Massachusetts 02129
Copyright• 1980 by Charles River Books, Inc.

ISBN 0 89182 018 3
Library of Congress Card Number 80-10986

For Mary and Roy, Peg and Gerard

CONTENTS

ILLUSTRATIONS

IT WILL TAKE A LIFETIME

PART ONE

PATRICK

The yellow light hurt my eyes. My cousin Margaret Kellet was standing in the doorway saying, "Your mother wants you to come downstairs." At the other bed my brother Gerard was putting on his clothes.

"I don't want to get up," I said.

"You'd better come," Margaret said. "You may never see your daddy again." We never called him daddy; we called him Pa or Father. Mother called him Patrick, or rarely, and only she, Packie.

There were cousins and neighbors in the darkened parlor and dining room. From the bedroom I heard my Mother saying the prayers for the dying. My Father lay with his eyes closed, breathing hard. At intervals my Mother wiped the foam from his lips with a linen napkin. His breathing came slower, and Mother said, "Patrick, will you bless the children?" Starting with John, the eldest, then Mary, Paula, Anne Therese, Gerard, and me, we knelt beside him and he lifted his hand to our foreheads.

My Grandfather, Cornelius Sweeney, was eight when he landed in Boston on May 30, 1849. The sailing ship *Argyll* had brought him from Cork with his mother Johanna, his sister Ellen, and his brothers John and Dennis.

They had told the immigration official that they were coming to America to work; after each of their names on the ship's passenger list was written the word "labor."

In the Fort Hill section of Boston, within walking distance of Long Wharf, where they landed, Cornelius started to learn tailoring. Soon they moved to Milford, a little town thirty miles west of Boston. Dennis died at Fredericksburg in the uniform of the 40th

3

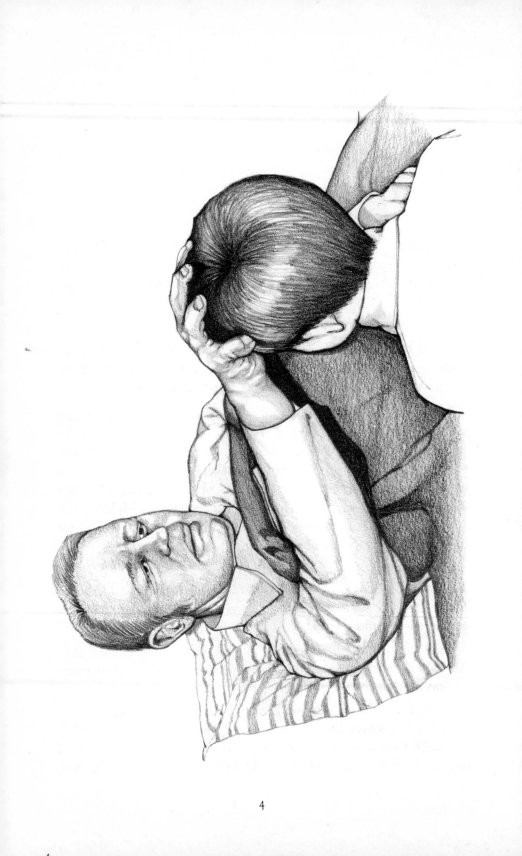

New York Volunteers.

Cornelius worked for some years at making boots. Then he opened a meat market on sloping Central Street, near the intersection with Main Street. This was Milford's business section: a few clothing stores, groceries, livery stables, and lodge halls. Much of the town's business was done by peddlers. Off the tailboard of the butcher cart he sold hams, legs of lamb, steaks, sausage, and tripe.

When the market on Central Street was burned out, Cornelius built another, a white clapboarded building in the yard of the house he had bought at 44 Pearl Street. As the first Irish in a Yankee neighborhood, Cornelius and his wife, sweet Margaret Lenihan, and their six children, were not welcome. The family next door put up a fence topped with barbed wire.

Cornelius spoke to his neighbor across the fence. "My children will never harm your property, and someday they'll own it." He was right. When Patrick, my Father, married Ellen McQuaid in 1901, he built the house at 42 Pearl Street, where I was born.

When Patrick was a sophomore at Milford High, Grandfather took him out of school to work in the market. Patrick threw himself on the high school lawn and sobbed. He hadn't been shaken by such grief since his mother's death. For two years he thought he would go back, but he never did.

He loved books; he read Dickens in cheap editions with crabbed type when he was a child, then went on to biography and history. He went to night school to learn French. For some years he was chairman of the town library board. He avoided politics. I don't recall his ever speaking in town meeting, although he must have risen to give the report on the library. Milford used the dog-license fees to buy books; the library flourished or waned with the dog population.

Once three grave Yankee gentlemen urged him to run for selectman. "We have wintered and summered you," one of them said. He declined.

The market prospered, and with a partner he opened a second market on Main Street. Though he was always tired from over-work, he was a supremely happy man.

Early Sunday mornings, when he should have been sleeping, we younger children would come down from our rooms and climb on our parents' bed. We crawled over his chest, pulled his ear lobes, ran our fingers over the sandpaper on his chin.

We were expected to work. From the age of six I was around the market, bagging potatoes in pecks and half-pecks, delivering meat orders in the neighborhood.

He lived until he was fifty. He survived his first attack and awoke the next morning. "I thought I had died," he said. "There's nothing to it." He lingered on for some months.

At the hour of his funeral the stores along Main Street closed. His friends, Dr. John Gallagher, William Ring, his partner William Quirk, Dr. Tom Nugent, Judge John Lynch and Judge John E. Swift walked beside him into the crowded church. Stand-ing at his grave I could see the Charles River where he had skated and swum as a boy.

A few days before my Father's death the parish priest came to bring him Holy Communion. As the youngest, I met the priest at the door with a lighted candle, and conducted him to Father's room. There I said the Latin *confiteor*, which I had learned in order to qualify as a Mass-server. He was quite weak now, and miserable with pain in the side of his head.

Before I left for school the nurse said my Father wanted to speak to me. As I stood beside him, he opened his eyes and looked at me for a moment, and said, "Thank you." He was thanking *me*.

It will take a lifetime to reply.

MORNING

"I could die waltzin'," my Father said. In fact, he was a poor dancer, with a tendency to hop. Mother, who loved dancing, married him for other qualities.

She grew up in Boston, he in Milford, a town thirty miles out in the country. Each summer Mother spent some weeks in Milford with Auntie Peard, Grandfather McQuaid's first cousin. She was the widow of Robert Peard, who had died in the Civil War. Mrs. Peard survived him for more than thirty years, living on a pension that gave her modest comfort in a little house in the center of town.

He had died in camp, probably of typhoid, while McClennan was honing a fine edge on the Army of the Potomac. Peard had been the Lieutenant Colonel commanding the Ninth Massachusetts Regiment, who marched under the green flag of Ireland. It worried Mrs. Peard that Milford might forget its hero, and on a spring day, with the GAR parading in their black uniforms with gold buttons, and gold acorns on their hatbrims, she presented his unblooded sword to the town.

Mother was born in the South End of Boston, and grew up in a bow-fronted brick house on Massachusetts Avenue. In her teens they moved out to Dorchester, to a house on Edson Street where there were apple trees in the yard and where Mother could ride her bicycle in the quiet streets.

The Curley family lived nearby, in Fellows Court. Grandfather McQuaid set up John Curley and my Uncle William McQuaid in the grocery business in Dorchester. The store never prospered, and Grandfather's opinion was that the young partners had spent too much time at the baseball games.

At any rate, John Curley lived a long and useful life, somewhat overshadowed by his younger brother, James Michael, who went into politics. My Uncle William came to a tragic end. He worked for the Boston Edison, and one day fell into some uncovered machinery. His body was terribly mangled when they dug it out of the cogwheels.

In the summers in Milford, Mother made many friends. One of them was Maggie Ross, whose father, Peter Ross, owned granite quarries in the Deerbrook section of Milford. There were joyous summer occasions at the Ross farmhouse, when friends and a numerous cousinry would gather for a clambake.

This called for a careful ritual. A hole was dug in a nearby field and a fire lit over fieldstones in the bottom of the hole. About noon the embers were raked out and in went potatoes, clams, lobsters, ears of corn, between layers of wet seaweed on the hot stones. A square of canvas covered the primitive pressure cooker.

When Peter Ross's watch indicated that the food was ready, the bake hole was uncovered and the steaming treasure spread on trestle tables, with chowder brought from the farm kitchen, and crocks of pickles and bowls of hot butter, corn bread and saleratus biscuits, and hard common crackers for the chowder.

Afterwards there would be music around the harmonium as Mother played and everyone sang. At the end of the day Father squired her home in the democrat, to Auntie Peard's house on Granite Street.

Father's younger brother John, a seminarian at St. Mary's in Baltimore, had promised to officiate at Father's marriage, but died before ordination. Father, in his intense grief, thought perhaps he was called to take John's place in the priesthood. He spent a night in prayer in the parish church, and came home in the morning with his decision made.

Auntie Peard and Mother were visiting in Newport and Father came down from Milford. He and Mother saw the great houses on Bellevue Avenue, and walked along the lovely cliffs. In Touro

Park, near the Norman Tower, they became engaged.

During the winter months Father often went into Boston on the Boston and Albany, and took the horsecar out to Dorchester. Once he peddled into Boston on his bike, but he never was much of a cyclist. The bike came back to Milford in the baggage car.

After Notre Dame Academy and Bryant and Stratton's, Mother was employed as a secretary to the president of the Fraternal Life Insurance Company on State Street. She took letters in Pitman shorthand and typed out endless letters to clients, which always began, "Dear Sir and Brother," and ended, "Yours in P. H. and P." This meant peace, health, and prosperity.

When Mother ordered her wedding invitations from M.T. Bird, the elderly clerk said, "It will mean much to you socially, Miss, to have your wedding stationery from Bird's." This amused Mother considerably; the orbit of society didn't touch either Edson Street or Milford. Aunt Mary McQuaid, a milliner on Tremont Street, took a dim view of the whole matter. "All that education to marry a country butcher," she said.

They were married in St. Matthew's in Dorchester, and there was a reception on Edson Street under the apple trees. For their honeymoon they took the train to Buffalo, where there was a world's fair in progress and, of course, Niagara nearby. They lived in a flat in Milford the first year, while Father was having a house built on Pearl Street.

They didn't travel much ever after, but Mother did attend the Eucharistic Congress in Montreal in 1910, after the four older children were born. She and her close friend, Dora Lynch, were there only a few days when newspaper reports from Montreal of sentiment against the United States caused Father and Judge John Lynch to worry about possible riots. John Lynch sent a telegram to Dora expressing their fears and ending with the request, "Return at once."

Well, they did, but I'm not sure that they came exactly at once. It takes more than a possible riot to pry two devout ladies loose from a Eucharistic Congress.

A HOUSE ON PEARL STREET

When I was four and my brother Gerard eight, I was jealous of him because he could read. It was an accomplishment that was not allowed to lie fallow—he had to read the newspaper to Grandfather. Grandfather was enjoying the last few months of his life propped up in his bed in the old homestead, with his wisp of beard protruding over the top of the white bedspread.

It was said that Gerard read him everything in the six-page Milford *Daily News*, including corset ads and shipwreck notices that ran: "My wife having left my bed and board, I will not be liable for bills contracted by her after this date." Grandfather would listen gravely, sometimes with his eyes closed, but he would come fully awake if he detected a word mispronounced.

One day I heard Gerard reading the "Milford Minor Notes," a column of mixed news and one-line ads that was the compendium of the town's social life. This is what he read:

"Manning's shoes wear well."

"Battery service at Bullard's."

"If moving call Ritz Company."

"The Excell for a real marcel."

"The Christian Endeavor will have a covered-dish supper at the parsonage tomorrow night. Bring dishes and silver."

"Mr. William Bollestor is breaking in a new six-cylinder Franklin touring car."

"The Misses Thayer motored to Nantasket Beach yesterday, taking as their guest Miss Mary O. Sumner."

"Mr. and Mrs. Patrick L. Manning are vacationizing this week in Providence, and taking side trips to points of interest."

"Mr. Peachy Casasanta is accepting pupils for pianoforte and clarinet."

"Mr. William Ring is recovering at his home on West Street from a SEVere cold."

"SevERE!" Grandfather said, opening one eye. "Don't you know how to pronounce?"

Then Grandfather slept, and Gerard took the opportunity to wander downstairs, knowing that Hannah, our unmarried aunt, had just taken a cake from the oven. She had one cake recipe which she had learned from her mother and she had rightly never seen any reason to change. It produced a golden yellow cake with frosting made of granulated sugar, bitter chocolate, and butter. Aunt Hannah cut a piece of cake and poured a glass of milk for Gerard, swatted a fly that had invaded her kitchen, and sternly ordered the cat off the Boston rocker.

"Tell me about Grandfather," Gerard said. We had heard it all before, but we enjoyed hearing the story, and could always ask for more details.

Grandfather had come from Cork at the age of eight and had shortly begun to "peg boots" as his relatives did. This was a farm industry. There were little workshops in the farmyards, where every week a jobber would deliver bales of leather and boxes of wooden pegs, and pick up the half-made boots to be finished in the shop in town. Working all day until the light failed, the men and boys would build the boots on the metal lasts, pegging in the soles.

Grandfather saved his money and became a peddler of "meats and provisions" from a paneled butcher-wagon in the farms and villages around Milford. Then he bought the house on Pearl Street, where his children were to grow up and where he now lived. In the wide yard he built the white clapboard market.

He was a wiry, aggressive man, full of the zest of work and life, with a melting tenderness for his grandchildren. When my Father, having served his apprenticeship on the butcher-wagon, took over the expanding business, Grandfather had no responsibilities except sitting in the sun, lighting his pipe, and expressing his convictions about the lineage of Kaiser Wilhelm II.

He stoutly resisted the telephone, but when Father, who always addressed Grandfather as Sir, had one installed in the market anyhow, Grandfather developed a liking for it. When he helped on busy days he answered the telephone as often as possible.

Aunt Hannah and Grandfather had sailed to England and Ireland just before the World War. We knew that chapter by heart: Grandfather climbing to the Whispering Gallery in St. Paul's, and walking the Roman Wall at Chester; Grandfather at Clontarf and Gendalough and Glengariff, putting his hand on Daniel O'Connell's coffin at Glasnevin, running up the hill at Ballincollig like a boy, with tears on his face, to find the cottage he had quitted for America sixty years before.

"Boy, where are you?" Grandfather spoke from upstairs.

"Here, Grandfather!" Gerard called out, and he quickly finished the milk and ran up to where the old man lay like a dying king borne to a headland to look out to sea.

REMEMBERING MUSIC

We were a musical family except for the two youngest, Gerard and me. We hadn't an ounce of music between us. Gerard had indulged a fleeting attraction to the trumpet, and I "took piano" for a year before Mother allowed us to stop the half-hearted effort.

Mine was a defect of concentration. Mother declared that Gerard's antipathy to music had set in early. He was normally a cheerful and self-reliant infant, but when in the early dusk before the older children had come in huntsman-hungry, and before Father had come home from the market, Mother would sit down at the piano, Gerard would bellow indignantly.

The other four children made up for our lack of talent. John, the eldest, under the truculent instruction of a teacher named Professor Wenzel, became an excellent violinist. Mary was a mezzo-soprano and played the piano with dashing competence. The 'cello was Paula's choice, a small girl who drew lovely ruminations from the big instrument. Anne played the violin seriously and the piano tentatively.

None of them could hold a candle to Mother. She had been educated at the Boston Academy of Notre Dame in Berkeley Street and would recall the tedious hours of practice at scales and chords, and the exacting progress through the classics.

In her senior year, on Prize Day, with the tired old archbishop, John Joseph Williams, as guest of honor, Mother and another girl had sat back to back at grand pianos and played Karl Maria von Weber's rococo, "Invitation to the Dance." The Hallet and Davis upright that dominated our parlor had been Grandfather Mc-Quaid's graduation gift.

We never had a Victrola, and were the last family on Pearl street to buy a radio. But there was music in the house from breakfast onwards. We spent our spare money on sheet music, and even in straitened times the piano was tuned regularly by Mr. Coulliard, the blind piano-tuner. It was a wondrous procedure for a small boy to watch: Mr. Coulliard crashing the keys and tightening the wires in the exposed innards of the piano, then polishing the ebony panels before accepting his fee and a glass of lemonade.

Milford loved music. There was a succession of choral societies, flourishing choirs in the churches, band concerts on Town Park, and innumerable children aspiring to various instruments at a dollar a lesson.

Once the Irish tenor, John McCormack, sang in Town Hall in a setting of Doric simplicity. The only stage decoration was a sign reading, "No Spitting," and another saying, "Charleston Dance Not Permitted in This Hall."

One of the fine things the VFW did for the town was to sponsor a drum and bugle corps. Any youngster could join, and more than a hundred did. The VFW bought the drums and bugles and fitted out the corps with white sailor suits. If memory serves, they played three tunes, repeating them as they marched through the streets on spring days, preparing for the parades on Memorial Day and the Fourth of July.

On holiday evenings we had family concerts, for ourselves and for any neighbors who might wander in. They were celebrations of family pride and of an instinct as old as the tribe. We sang songs like "Tenting Tonight," "Seeing Nellie Home," "The Lost Chord," and "The Meeting of the Waters."

Mother played Schubert, reading the music intently while Father turned the pages. Then John would oblige with "The Flight of the Bumblebee" and Paula and Anne and Mother would play "Meditation from Thaïs." Mary played and sang Gounod's *Ave Maria*, and then gave us a sparkling torrent of jazz that

15

brought applause from neighbors on nearby piazzas.

For a finale, and for a memory still resonant, we would stand around Mother at the piano, with Father beside her, and sing Carrie Jacobs Bond's "A Perfect Day."

In a way, it was.

ADIN BALLOU AND THE ORTHODOX DOG

Last year, when I observed the twenty-fifth anniversary of my ordination, my high school classmate, Charlie Smith, gave me a valuable gift. It is Adin Ballou's *History of Milford*, published on the occasion of the town's centenary in 1880. The book is handsomely bound in tan calf, and weighs 4½ pounds.

The Reverend Mr. Ballou, then in his seventy-eighth year, was pastor of the Universalist Church. I don't believe Adin missed a single item of local history, and he had participated in much of it. Since he had preached his first sermon at the age of eighteen he had solemnized one thousand marriages.

I have been digging into the book at odd times and have found some delightful nuggets. One is about the Orthodox Dog. The dog's name is unfortunately not given; it belonged to the Clark family, whose farm lay a mile out of town. In my childhood the Clarks, two generations later, sold us milk and excellent russet cider.

"Mr. Clark and family," Ballou related, "had a remarkable dog,—scarcely less pious than the rest of the household, especially in attendance on public worship, and deportment during the services. . . . As surely as Sunday came and the Congregational bell rang, he gravely proceeded to church and posted himself directly under the pulpit. There he remained during the services, invariably rising to his feet, as the congregation did, for singing, prayer, and benediction, and the rest of the time quietly sitting on his haunches, or lying recumbent."

When the rival Universalist Church added its deep-toned bell to the Sunday morning chime, the dog took no notice, but remained steadfast in his Congregational allegiance through a long life.

This matter of religious preference among dogs is not as rare as my readers may think. Some Methodist neighbors of ours had a nervous Labrador retriever who sometimes bit the mailman. The mailman forgave the dog in a Christian spirit, but had no doubt of the animal's motivation. "He bites me," the mailman said, "because I'm a Baptist."

The question has been raised whether cats have any religious inclinations. I regret to say that they have not. But my family once owned a cat, a large yellow creature named Fifi, who had a keen sense of morality which she frequently expressed. (Scholars are agreed that cats understand everything that humans say, though, like computers, they have some difficulty with the subjunctive.)

Mother did not allow us to bring animals into the house, not even a lost dog or a harmless snake, but was prevailed on to tolerate Fifi on the claim that the cat was an efficient mouser. This was not true. Occasionally Fifi would dart into the pantry and sniff around the baseboards. It meant nothing. When there was evidence of mice we had to buy a mousetrap.

Fifi spent most of her time sleeping or foraging for meat scraps in the neighborhood market Father kept next door to our house. Her preference was for calves' liver, but she wasn't fussy.

Her fussiness was expressed only in an abhorrence to strong language. We had a cousin, an old gentleman in his eighties called Uncle Martin, who was much beloved by my parents. Occasionally he would come out from Boston on the train, the "steam cars," for a day's visit. He would sit in our parlor, his hands on the top of his cane, recalling old times.

When he reached the denouement of his stories he would exclaim, "Be hell and be damn," which was his only resort to profanity. Fifi would immediately leave the room.

Once at the supper table, when we were reciting jingles and telling riddles, Father said:

A wonderful bird is the pelican -

His beak can hold more than his belly can.
He can keep in his beak
Enough food for a week,
Though I don't know how the hell he can.

Fifi disappeared for three days. I think she was outraged because Father was the only person in the household she respected.

On the third day of her absence one of our cousins in Upton called up to ask if Fifi were missing; in fact she had been staying with them for two days. Fifi was acquainted with them because on some Sunday afternoons she had come along in the flivver when we had gone visiting.

Mother suggested that if they had a mind to keep Fifi it would be perfectly all right, but the offer was declined. Fifi was spending her time sleeping or meowing for food. One of the market clerks was sent to pick her up in the flivver. Fifi returned sleeping in the back seat.

For a while she seemed to regret her hasty action, and would rub up against our legs and purr; she attempted unsuccessfully to jump up on Father's lap.

I think that about this time Fifi realized that she had worn out her welcome. One day she disappeared again. A neighbor of ours, a small boy who was known to make up stories but who this time crossed his heart and hoped to die, reported that he had seen our cat jump up on a wagon. It belonged to a man who drove down our street once every spring selling ladders and wicker chairs. He came from Woonsocket, Rhode Island.

Perhaps Fifi amused her new family with her mouse-detection act, and her moral standards, meanwhile eating them out of house and home.

But I have wandered too far from Reverend Mr. Ballou's history. It was well-known that Universalists do not believe in hell. No one ever blamed them for this notion, especially since all the Universalists we knew were clearly not headed there anyhow. But gentle old Adin was willing to extend the doctrine of universal reconciliation. He finished his story of the Orthodox Dog by saying, "Surely such a dog, if animals have immortality, ought to have a place among the blest."

A FIND ON GOODSPEED'S BARGAIN TABLE

Down a few steps from snow-encumbered Milk Street, a time ago, I entered Goodspeed's, stamping snow from my boots so as not to leave puddles between the book stacks.

Among the dozen or so bookstores I know, most of them are strongly lighted and pastel-walled, and the books are fresh from the printer. The book jackets are colored emblems of their contents, like tavern signs: The Swan and Bottles, The Green Dragon, The Prospect of Whitby.

Goodspeed's confounds the Peter-Panism of our culture, and listens for the tick-tock of time. There is not a new book in the store, hardly a book jacket that is not scuffed or faded.

I came in partly to escape the harbor wind, partly to greet a clerk who is a friend of mine, partly to keep an open mind on the purchase of a second-hand book. I've had good luck on several occasions. For ten cents I purchased *A Gourmet's Guide to Europe*, a small volume bound in red calf, written by a British colonel whose name escapes me, and published about 1910.

Besides the recollections of satisfactory meals the colonel had eaten on Her Majesty's service, there are comments on society. "Portugal," he informs us, "is the kingdom of the frying pan." And he remarks on the exemplary hospitality shown by the Kaiser to British officers who happen to be in Kiel during the regatta.

Another find was *Birds of the Boston Public Garden*, by Horace W. Wright. It describes 116 varieties of birds seen on the Public Garden during the years 1900 to 1908. Few human foibles are as innocent and consoling as bird-watching. There is a touching seriousness about this chronicle as endearing as stereopticon views or scrimshaw sculpture.

"On May 18, 1908," Wright tells us, "an olive-backed thrush in a beech which stands near the Everett statue sang without ceasing for a half-hour or more, quite as he would have sung in a White Mountain forest such as he loves so well. When I had passed through the grounds and returned again to the vicinity of the beech tree, the bird was still singing."

The 25-cent table near the door displayed the residue of the bookseller's barrel. Here were novels by Mrs. Humphrey Ward and Warwick Deeping, thick reports on an agronomy fifty harvests past, little handbooks on Renaissance sculpture, with muddy half-tones.

I picked up a book bound in marbled boards, with a tan leather spine stamped in gold. It was volume nine of *Half-Hours with the British Poets*. The spotted flyleaf bore a name familiar to me from old letters, and the date, 1892, was right. It was signed "Henry McQuaid," and with a lift of the heart I recognized the hand of a granduncle whom I had never seen.

My Grandfather's people were of a kind you might call working class affluent, whom the Boston novelists have neglected. Immigrants, and the children of immigrants, they combined zest for work with a clear view of the main chance, and a hunger for education. None of Henry McQuaid's generation made it to college, but they attended night classes, they swelled the audiences on the lecture circuit, they were familiar with the culture of books.

They were good citizens, I suspect, of an Irish Puritan kind. One of them had been a young lieutenant colonel commanding the Ninth Massachusetts Volunteers. Another was a flautist in the Boston Symphony Orchestra. My Grandmother sang in the Handel and Haydn.

I believe Henry McQuaid was a machinist, as my Grandfather was, and a bachelor. Family lore links him with my grandaunt, Mary McQuaid, who was a milliner with a shop on Tremont

Street.

Several times Mary traveled to Paris to attend the fashion shows and bring home ideas. Once, when Mary was abroad, Henry received a cablegram from her which read simply, "Come." Everyone agreed that he must go at once to rescue her from whatever straits she had fallen into in a city like Paris. He took the next boat for Le Havre.

Shortly after his departure, a letter came from Mary saying she was minded to return by way of New York, landing on a particular day, and that if the plan eventuated she would ask Henry to meet her by sending him a one-word cablegram.

Finding his sister already embarked, Henry saw Paris and some other cities, and lost a few francs at Monte Carlo.

The only thing I know about Granduncle Henry is that towards the end of his life he became obsessed with the stock market, and put all his money into worthless stocks. Eventually he sold his library, carrying the books in suitcase loads to the second-hand bookshops. I wish I knew more about him than these few memories, and the lonely grave in Old Calvary, and a book on the bargain table at Goodspeed's.

A BACKWARD EDUCATION

It must be admitted that I had a backward education. Let me see. Macaulay died in 1859, the same year as Washington Irving. Carlyle passed over in 1881. Edmund Burke flourished in the eighteenth century, and John Milton in the seventeenth. Virgil and Cicero and Caesar were gathered to their fathers before the Census of Augustus.

We read them, we the children of factory hands, farmers, and country butchers. We puzzled out the Latin verbs, measured the hexameters, looked up the archaic English as if we were the sons of landed gentry preparing to go up to Balliol.

We studied Latin to learn the mechanics and the texture of language, and to learn how effects challenge causes. And because, as Jaime Castiello has said, you sharpen a blade on stone, not on wood.

Four years of Latin, of English, of Christian Doctrine; three of French; two of history, besides shorter skirmishes with algebra, plane geometry, chemistry, and physics. The curriculum had been shortened; my elder brother and sister had studied Greek and solid geometry.

It was hard work, it was boring, it was magnificent.

The teaching was middling to excellent: strong in Latin, English and math; wooly in science, poor and then good in French. When I started French in the tenth grade my Mother was troubled at the French accent I brought home, almost as much as she had been when, in the fourth grade, I brought home lice in my hair.

Yet I received a respectable mark in the tenth grade for a paper offering my conclusions that the Spanish Inquisition was a mean and foolish business. When I think of elegance of style I remember Edmund Burke's "On Conciliation With the Colonies," which we read aloud in senior year.

Poetry was a mixed catch. We read "Barbara Frietchie," Poe, Longfellow, and Lars Porsena of Clusium, -but Milton too. My first recognition of the classic music in poetry came with "L'Allegro," "Il Penseroso," and "Lycidas," which I read in the eleventh grade.

Though much of what was taught was lost on us, we were shown the best. We were not coddled ignorance; whoever drew up the curriculum knew the workable strategies against that.

Jean Mayer, President of Tufts University, recently observed in *Saturday Review*: "It may well be that educationists and drafters of curricula will someday evolve a teaching scheme more comprehensive, more inspiring, more sophisticated than a classical education was for us. But it has not happened yet." And the *Harvard Gazette* quotes David Riesman's remark that when he reads a student's paper that shows organization and ease with language, he suspects that the student has come from a school with a name like St. Catherine's or St. Xavier's.

My high school was St. Mary's in Milford, Massachusetts. The Principal was John P. Donahue, a curate in the parish. Father Donahue was an exemplary parish priest, with the one weakness of an apocalyptic preaching style. He denounced Communism at the narrowest opportunity. I am glad to report that Communism never gained a foothold in Milford.

He found his Camelot in the high school. He gave a weekly lecture on religion, coached the debating teams, moderated football, basketball, and the speech forum, got us out of court or into college.

The teachers were Sisters of St. Joseph. Sister Rose Concepta, who taught Latin, English, and French, is the only one who survives, in her eightieth year.

She goaded us out of the flânerie of senior year to bell the lion of college entrance examinations. I remember the tiring daily review of Latin grammar, and the taste of winsome prose in English class. She had learned her French by the book, and distrusted her own accent. Half the French period was spent in listening to language records.

What are the great teacher's gifts? Intelligence, and love for the job, and the conviction that literature, the treasure she has made her own, must be opened to its unlikely heirs. Every day her enthusiasm challenged us to come along to see what we would see. Only rarely, once a season at most, a Celtic gloom darkened her radiance, perhaps when she thought too much about the odds that she faced.

Against my will, at violence to my juvenile hedonism, I discovered some fragments of wisdom; enough, at least, to show me that learning can tranform life. It is not too late to say thank you.

SUMMER

There was never a handsomer beach than Nantasket, never a more joyous amusement park than Paragon, never a happier summer than that one, when I was six.

We had been to Nantasket before on day trips. We had a Buick touring car which, loaded with brothers and sisters and cousins, baskets of sandwiches and hard-boiled eggs, two watermelons, sand pails and swimming gear, and jars of cocoa butter, made the forty-mile trip from Milford. Aunt Hannah, Father's elder sister came along to keep order, to warn against sunburn, and to count children before the trip home.

Hannah enjoyed the sea breeze and, I think, thought there was something curative about it. As we approached the shore she would exhort us to "smell the salt air." There is a domestic legend that on one trip she gave this advice in Medway, three miles out of Milford.

That summer my parents hired Harvey Trask's cottage at Nantasket for the month of July. Mr. Trask kept a bicycle shop in Milford. It was one of the more attractive establishments on Main Street, a favorite of small boys who stared in the window at the ranks of red and chrome bicycles, a few tandems and one four-seater hung up on the back wall of the store.

Trask's cottage was seven rooms and a screened piazza on two sides. I never smell new wood or a balky oil stove without remembering that cottage. It was on Atlantic Hill, between Paragon Park and the ocean, where the lower beach curved out to a rocky headland. The slope grew wild with hay and buttercups and the blue flowers we called bachelor's button.

In the middle distance one of the peaks of the Paragon Park roller coaster rose over the cottage roofs. If the wind was from the west we could hear the gears clicking as the cars made the steep ascent, and the screams of the passengers as the cars swooped down the terrible drop. A boy in the neighborhood said that there was an even higher roller coaster at Revere, a beach north of Boston. A sailor had stood up in a car and had had his neck broken, the boy said proudly.

We six children settled in, chose our sleeping places, hung our Sunday clothes in closets and found a path to the beach. Elizabeth O'Brien, our cousin who was a nurse on vacation, looked after us, and Mrs. Caroline Lindgren, who helped Mother on weekends, cooked our meals.

As one of a pack of children, or alone, I roamed the great beach, and found mussel shells and armored crabs and razor clams, and starfish in the rock pools. On the horizon's line, ships inched by.

In and out of the water at all hours, I began to learn the power of the sea, the power to destroy and to heal. "Smell the salt air," Aunt Hannah said. I have remembered it long afterward, when the salt smell of the tides, and the owl's hoot of foghorns, and the dressage of gulls on the rough wind have brought me peace.

Paragon Park at night was a tumult of light and plunking music and whirling motion. Thought I was forbidden the roller coaster, I tried the other rides—the Dodge-ems and the Red Mill frequently. The Flying Horses was the most stirring. To mount the wooden horse and grasp the reins and then to feel the whole marvelous contraption set in motion to the blare of the calliope was to make real all the cowboy dreams of childhood.

Between the leaping horses were settees—golden thrones or red chairs ornamented with carved dragons—where grown-ups could ride if they had a mind to. My brother Gerard asked Mrs. Lindgren whether she would like to ride on the merry-go-round. She said she would. I remember what a figure of dignity she made, a gray-haired lady in a dragon's chair going around and around on

the carousel.

Our parents came down from Milford on weekends. On Friday afternoon we would wait for them on the Nantasket Pier until the Boston boat, the *Allerton* or the *Dorothy Standish*, warped into the pier and the deckhands slid out the gangplank. Then they appeared, Father in a straw boater and a gray suit, Mother in her blue chambray dress. We conducted them in a flurry of competing conversation along the wharf to Nantasket Avenue and up Atlantic Hill.

In my Father's house there are many mansions. Perhaps there is one like this—a cottage within sound of the ocean, with the sweet night air murmurous with crickets, and my parents asleep in a room upstairs.

MASS OF THE POOR

My Mother's voice came thinly through the dark, and I responded sleepily, swinging my feet out of the warm cocoon of bedclothes. The straw matting was cold and smooth under my feet. It was a wintry five o'clock, and I had been up that early only a few times before.

A rooster crowed somewhere, a skyrocket of sound. I did not know of anyone within a mile who raised poultry, but sometimes very early in the morning I would hear this insolent fanfare.

I hurried into my clothes and let myself out of the silent house. Down the street there were lights in the rectory and a cab stood waiting, the driver smoking sleepily and not caring. "Get in and wait," he said, snorting the smoke from his nostrils. "He'll be out in a minute."

The door of the rectory opened and the priest came carefully down the steps and hurried down the walk, pulling on his gloves.

"Good morning, Father," I said, and the driver touched his cap and started the car. Main Street was dark as we came through, except for a lunch room that was full of yellow light; the windows were steamed so we couldn't see inside. At a traffic light blinking yellow we turned west and headed out of town.

"Sure you got everything, Father?" the driver said, making conversation.

"Everything is all set," the priest said. "I was up there last night." He was sitting in the back with his gloved hands on his knees. The trees and houses as we passed were black armatures against the rose window of dawn. A rooster crowed triumphantly, close by now, for we were riding through the fields and thin

woods that border the Grafton road.

We turned into Asylum Street, a narrow whimsical track that went diagonally across a wooded hillside, looping and turning to skirt a gully or an outcropping of shale. Clumps of sumac, as startlingly red as the skirts of Connemara women, were the only color in the shadowy woods. A line of telegraph poles, weathered grey as pewter, followed the road by angular fits and starts.

The cab emerged near the top of the ridge, where a white clapboarded farmhouse stood on the sloping lawn with a faded red barn beside it and a silo trussed with rusty steel cables. Every window in the upper floor of the farmhouse was lighted, though now it was full dawn and the sun was coming up, the edge of a wafer of light searing the top of the ridge.

The priest left his coat and hat in the bare parlor and went up the creaking stairs, with the Master of the Poor Farm, a large, nervous man in his shirtsleeves, clattering ahead of him in heavy shoes. In an angle of the corridor the vestments were spread on a table. The Master of the Poor Farm gave me a wooden match with an orange head and I went into the room where the makeshift altar was. I nicked the match into flame with my thumbnail and lit the candles, to murmurs of approval from the old people.

They were packed into the small room, seated in rows on kitchen chairs. Some sat staring at the floor, others were praying aloud; one man waved encouragement to me. A flood of pity and strange self-reproach rose from my belly and made my heart beat faster; they were a page out of the *Purgatorio*, a print of Hogarth's come to life. A few of the faces were familiar, and I recognized them as people I had thought were dead.

There was Joe-Edgar Garrity, a thin little man with a square chin who had always ridden a bicycle to work, his right leg clasped at the trouser cuff with a black tin clip. Joe would pedal by our house on his way to the straw-hat mill, bending over the handle bars like a seven-day bike racer. Here he was in this forgotten harbor of life, stooped and slow-gaited, stripped at last of all illusions of flight.

There was Stella Winters, who had worked in an office in Boston and had gone in and out each day on the train. Until middle life Stella had been a symbol of womanly success, rouged and fur-pieced, and high-heeled. Her friends had said of her, "Stella is so smart"; and her enemies had said, "She puts everything she earns on her back." She sat with her hands in her lap, in a blue house dress, her face blurred with age so that it looked like a squashed peach.

There was Mr. Shewring, a big-boned, formal man who had leaned a little from habitual courtesy. I remembered that his corded neck had been gyved with a gates-ajar collar, his bearded chin lifted, like Patmore's in the painting. His face had worn the curves of convinced mirth, a secret joke he would never share with anyone. There was no clue to it except the odor like vanilla extract that hung upon him. Now he wore no collar or tie, and the bristles were silver on his cheeks.

The heat eddied and boiled in the room and the air was barbed with the aggressive stink of disinfectant.

In the blood-red vestments of the Sacrifice, and carrying the caparisoned chalice with one hand, the priest edged his way slowly through the crowd. He set his burden on the altar, a blunted gable of red silk, and arranged the faded ribbons of the missal. I brushed against wasted shins as I bent to answer his *confiteor*. There were ancient faces at my elbow as I offered the wine and water. It was like Mass in the catacombs, with the hunted and the doomed and the beaten-with-rods gathered around the secret altar.

Since they had been told not to rise or kneel, and there was not room for them to file up to the altar for Holy Communion, the priest came to them, carrying the golden cup of blessing down one crowded row and up another, giving the sacred Body to all the hostages of life, not omitting one weeping old woman, or one angry old man, or one simpleton who said, "Thank you" and chewed the Host. Not one was omitted.

A rooster crowed again as the priest was bringing his thumb to his forehead at the Last Gospel. I thought suddenly that the chronology of the Passion had become confused, but I could not say how, or by whom, or whether in the murmuring of the old people Peter wept.

FLIGHT

My memories of childhood have the strong lines and contrasting masses of color I see in modern stained glass. I remember my first sight of an airplane on the ground, and the details are as clear as an Evie Hone window.

I was an airplane nut, and read all the books on aircraft in the town library. Novels like *Wings*, movies like *Dawn Patrol*, with its elegant charade of chivalry and death, fascinated me, but I spent most of my interest on the technical side of flight. I revelled in the vocabulary: aileron, dihedral, camber, fuselage, even nomenclature, which one of my authors used constantly. I thought it was another part of the plane.

Flight seemed as miraculous as the discovery of fire, and the slow-poke ways of Packards, Buicks and Tin Lizzies appeared doomed like the horse-drawn pungs that still carried their loads of wood and ice in the winter streets.

I remember the attempt of Nungesser and Coli to fly from France to New York; and with pride recollected in tranquility long after, I remember the 21st of May, 1927. I was going by the firebarn on Main Street that afternoon when the fire alarm blew two blasts. That was the signal for the end of a fire, the start of a parade, or any event of civic importance.

I walked into the firebarn and spoke to a fireman who was sitting in front of the radiator of the big LaFrance pumper. He said solemnly, "The American flag has been carried across the Atlantic by air." That was the first time I had heard the name Lindbergh.

Occasionally planes would pass over the town, low enough to

cast a shadow. Children would run after them, and the youngest of us would cry out, "Give us a ride!"

One day a plane landed. It came low over Pearl Street and went north over the houses where Pearl became Purchase Street, and the houses were farther apart, some of them farm houses. It had landed on Chester Clark's field by the time a crowd of town kids had arrived pell mell and ecstatic on an idle August morning. Mr. Clark had driven down from the house in his buggy, and was standing talking to the aviators. The horse, with the checkrein loosed, was eating grass beside the plane.

As we streamed across the field and stood at a little distance (the propeller, we warned each other, could cut you in two), Mr. Clark got in the buggy and drove off to the vast door of the cowbarn.

It was a biplane built of brown wood, with two cockpits and small wheels like the wheels on a training bicycle. One of the aviators, in a soiled grey jumper, stood near the tail eating an apple. When a few of the town kids approached and touched the tail he told them profanely to get away.

The other aviator, dressed in leather puttees and tan riding breeches, with a leather helmet, stood near the propeller. He was slapping the pages of an oil-stained book.

"Milford!" he said to the man in the jumper. "When he said Milford I thought he meant Milford, New Hampshire."

"Tough luck," the man in the jumper said equivalently.

I was the kid nearest the man in the helmet since I was trying to read the make of the plane printed on a plate on the hood. It was a Waco.

The helmeted man threw the book into the forward cockpit and spoke to me. "Kid, do me a favor." He drew a half dollar from his breeches pocket. "Run downtown and get me two packs of Camels."

"I'm too small," I said. "They won't sell them to me."

"Say they're for your old man. You can keep the change."

"My Father smokes a pipe," I said.

"And get me a map of Massachusetts and Connecticut," the helmeted man said. "I saw a gas station about a mile down the line."

"A *what?*"

"A roadmap." But he turned impatiently and gave the half dollar to another boy who went off like a shot.

"Come right back," the helmeted man said. "What is your name?"

"Puddin' tame," the boy called over his shoulder, and kept going.

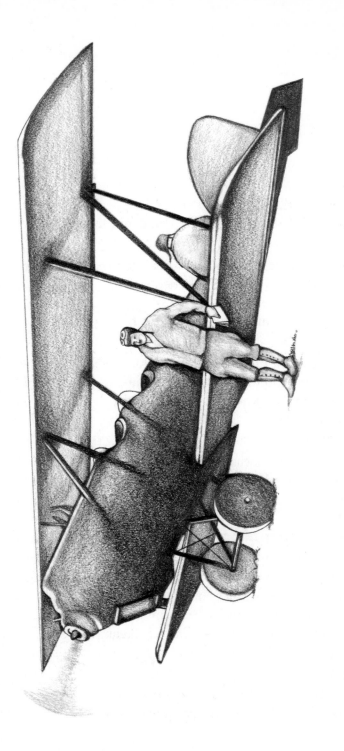

NEW YORK BY SEA

Before the tide of trade went out, before the wharves were abandoned to decay and the gulls, you could leave Boston by sea for nearly every port in the world.

The deep water of the harbor brought the great liners to the city's side. If you sat on the lichened wall at Castle Island you could see them going by. It was a procession that began back in the days when the merchantmen and the frigates dipped their flags to the red cross of St. George flying from the Castle.

When I was a boy and first saw this harbor, the sea-traffic had dwindled but there was still a sizable coastal trade. There were three sailings weekly to Portland, and two to Yarmouth, Nova Scotia. The ships of the Eastern Steamship Line left India Wharf on Monday, Wednesday, and Friday at 5 p.m.

Their timetable was fragrant with the poetry of town names: Rockland, Camden, Bucksport, Winterport, Bangor, with a connection for North Haven, Stonington, Southwest Harbor, Northeast Harbor, Seal Harbor, Bar Harbor, Dark Harbor, South Brooksville, Deer Isle, Brooklin, South Bluehill, Bluehill.

You had a couple of choices for going to New York. The Fall River Line had been lately discontinued, but you could sail from Providence (there was a boat train from Boston with a parlor car). The fare was $4.13, and staterooms cost $1.08, $1.62, and $2.16. The New York boats of the Eastern Steamship Line, named prosaically the *Boston* and the *New York*, left by turns each day from India Wharf.

I had been preparing for the voyage ever since I had been told some weeks before that I might make the trip to New York. I had gotten some expert advice from neighbors to whom I had confided my jubilant plans. Several of them said, "Look out for bad weather off Point Judith." Or, "It will be pretty rough off Point Judith."

As for coping with New York, I knew it would be smart to shun the Bowery, where the rough element could be found. I knew all about that because I had read numerous novels by Horatio Alger. *Jed the Poorhouse Boy* and *Adrift in New York* had made me familiar with the Bowery and Bleecker Street and Tony Pastor's Theater. I knew that visitors were in peril of pickpockets. Forewarned was forearmed. I carried my money in a metal case fastened to my belt.

Down Boston Harbor in the late afternoon, threading the islands with their little houses, naming the harbor forts, hearing the bellbuoys ringing in the sea's jostle, losing the city in mist and the colors of sunset—it was an experience that enriched childhood.

Inside, the dining saloon was all stiff white linen and polished nickel silver. The waiters in starched white coats glided about as sure-footed as leopards. At the sideboard a waiter uncovered a tureen and filled me a bowl. I dipped my nose into the ambrosial steam and ate the noble clam chowder.

"Do you expect rough weather off Point Judith?" I asked the waiter.

"Nossir," he replied.

Back on deck I found some of the passengers at the rail. We had come through the uplifted leaves of the Sagamore drawbridge and were moving at slow speed through the Cape Cod Canal. Cars clustered here and there on the Canal banks, their headlights gleaming like wreckers' lamps. Occasionally a car's horn would sound and the captain would reply with a blast from the ship's horn.

Snug in my bunk, smelling the salt-sweet sea, hearing the creaking of the timbers and the slap of the water on the hull, I slept. I was up early to see the harbor, the green shore of Long Island, and the towers of New York. There was the thick spire of the

Woolworth Building, and the apex of the Chrysler Building like the blade of a swordfish. There was Lady Liberty holding up her torch to enlighten the world.

I never saw the Bowery or the Battery or Chinatown that first day ashore in New York, but I rode a double decker bus up Fifth Avenue from Washington Square, and got as far as 241st Street for a dime. I discovered the armor and the mummies and bronze citizenry of Rodin at the Metropolitan, and the quaint Village with its Federalist streets and unexpected shows of paintings hanging on fences.

Under the debris of time, New York must still be as shining and innocent as it was that day.

FOOL'S ERRAND

Falmouth Heights is one of a cluster of beaches that fringe the sea pine and oak at the elbow of the bent arm of Cape Cod. I had been there with my Mother and godmother for a few weeks in the July after my freshman year at Holy Cross. In late August, I wanted to go back, and not for the sea air and mild water and the sunsets.

I had looked up Jim Cobb, my classmate, who had a summer job but was free to join me in the evenings. One of the places where we hung out was the Sandwich Depot, which served plate-spanning sandwiches and generous sodas and college ices.

One of the people Jim introduced me to was a girl with intense brown eyes, and brown hair that curled like a fiddlehead under the left side of her chin. Often she brushed the curl back on her neck and revealed a gold button in her earlobe.

She smiled at others' wit, and stirred her pink ice cream soda with a long spoon. The juke box filled the big room with Tommy Dorsey's doomsday trombone. I was incapable of small talk, a dunce on the dance floor, a rube among the tanned and crew-cut squires.

On the sidewalk outside the Sandwich Depot, where the streetlights threw patterns of maple leaves on the ground, there were shouted goodbyes and the sounds of cars starting up. I heard her tell some of her girl friends that she would be on the beach in mid-morning.

It rained, and I was due to leave Falmouth that afternoon.

I wanted to return in August, and wrote Jim Cobb to say when I would arrive. I thumbed down from Milford. I had a knapsack, and wore white buckskin shoes, green slacks and a white linen jacket I was fond of. When I took up my thumbing station on the Bellingham road, a friend passing by said I looked like a barber on a house call.

Becalmed in Mansfield between rides, I sent my Mother a postcard, saying I had arrived in Mansfield. She suffered such whimsies gladly.

Jim Cobb's mother had a room for me, and made me welcome. She was a widow who had brought up Jim and his two sisters through the lean Cape Cod winters. She taught a class in the primary school.

Next morning, I was at the beach and saw the girl at a distance. She and two other girls were basking in the sun like seals on a rock. They rubbed lotion on their long legs and drank from a red thermos. I didn't have the courage to approach them. Twice I went down to the water and swam around miserably. And I lay on the sand and tried to read a book.

When the fire whistle sang noon, the girls picked up their gear and came up the beach. As they passed me, the girl seemed to remember having met me somewhere. "Hel-lo!" she said, and I said hello, and that was the lost moment.

I took a long walk in the afternoon. There had been rumors of sharks being seen off Nobska Point, but they had turned out to be dogfish. The beach was lightly crowded. Children built Beau Geste forts at the water's edge, and some older kids started a raucous softball game. At the sea wall, a Good Humor truck did a land-office business.

The sea was a page from a Winslow Homer sketchbook. A sailboat tacked against the wind, showing its white hull and the red ploughshare of its keel. The sail cupped the wind like a hand dipping water from a spring. Two black ducks went by, flying very fast, as thin as javelins. Farther out, a working boat was followed by a taggle of gulls. At the stern, a man in a yellow oilskin apron was cleaning fish with quick flashes of a knife. The sunset spread crimson and rose all over the great sky. There was no sign of her at the Sandwich Depot that night.

Sleep came grudgingly. Though the land breeze blew freshly in my window, my skin was sore from all that sun.

She was at the beach the next day, in and out of the water. I sat on the sea wall and watched her swim far out and then come lazily back, doing a flutter kick. She ran glistening out of the surf, and put on a floppy pink hat when she rejoined her friends. She wore a blue bathing suit that rose to her throat but swooped low in back. I imagined myself dancing with her, my hand on her shoulder blades. Her skin would be as smooth as the inner faces of an almond.

I thumbed home that afternoon. As the car went north through Teaticket and Pocasset, and over the clattering timber floor of the Bourne Bridge, there was an unlooked-for surge of joy. I knew myself better than before, not regretting anything, realizing that wisdom sometimes comes from fool's errands like mine.

From Mansfield, I sent a card to Mrs. Cobb.

THE FIRST TIME I SAW GERMANY

When I graduated from Holy Cross in June, 1939, my family, by what financial legerdemain I never knew, gave me the gift of a European trip. All through my college years I had talked about visiting England. My family's generosity allowed me to extend the itinerary.

An organization called SITA, Students' International Travel Association, offered a 7-country tour by train for, I believe, $450, and I signed up for that. One of the countries was Liechtenstein, which we saw on one sleepy afternoon.

It wasn't the best time to visit Europe, but a letter from SITA assured our group that there would be no war that year. We were twelve men and women from ten universities who embarked on the old *Volendam* of the Holland-America Line on July first. It was a slow voyage—ten days to Plymouth. The ship was crowded with young people heading for various kinds of European tours by train and bus and *faltboot* and bike. There were classes in languages and customs, as well as movies and dancing and scavenger hunts, and three meals and three snacks a day. It was a welcome rest after the tension of senior year and commencement. All the ancient cities would come alive out of our textbooks—London, Oxford, The Hague, Cologne, Venice, Florence, Rome! And there would be no war that year.

There were four days of marvelous weather in London, with flowers brimming among the old stones. But uniforms were everywhere, and people asked the same question: Do you think there will be a war? The ugly snouts of anti-aircraft guns protruded through the treetops in Hyde Park, and there were recruiting posters over the couchant lions in Trafalgar Square.

The night before we entered Germany we gathered in the dining room of our small hotel in Amsterdam, after dinner had been cleared away, for a briefing by one of the professors who ran the SITA tours.

It was a sobering experience, but nothing to chill the bones. The briefing didn't touch our easy certitudes (France had the best army in Europe; Germany and Russia were mortal enemies), but reminded us that we would be guests in a totalitarian country. Don't photograph military installations, or equipment like tanks or aircraft. Don't criticize the government. Don't mention Hitler's name in public. (We agreed to call him Jim, as later we called Mussolini Mooseface, or Mike Murphy.)

We were asked to sign an agreement, probably required by the German consulate, that we understood that it was forbidden to carry printed matter of a political kind into Germany.

Next morning, towards noon, the train from Amsterdam crossed the German border and stopped at Emmerich. We opened our suitcases for the customs guards to poke through, declared our money, produced our passports. A pudgy official in a grasshopper green uniform went through the car gathering passports, and took them out to the train station. We waited.

A tall man of about thirty years, in the black uniform of the SS, with silver buttons and a silver swastika on his cap, lounged through the car, chatting with us in stilted English. He was the first of hundreds of SS men we were to see in Germany. There was always one standing in front of the railroad station and looking at the crowds when the train discharged us in a German city. We would see them goose-stepping in the Adolf Hitler Platz in Munich, swarming in Nuremberg, the Party city, greeting each other with the lifted-arm salute in cafés and Rhine-boats.

The passport officer returned and stood in the aisle of the car, our red-jacketed passports held against his chest with his left arm. In his right hand he waved a passport and announced: "There is an American woman here who does not have a German visa. She must return to Amsterdam."

47

The SS man took the passport out of his hand, glanced at the photograph, riffled the pages, and handed it back to the passport officer, saying something in German that sounded like, "Oh, it's all right," or "I don't mind."

Without a word the passport control officer handed back all the passports.

Then we knew. The Party ran Germany. The Party dominated every surface and depth of German life, every instrument of government and folkway, every voice that might be raised in protest or in pain.

The genial SS man wished us a good journey; at the door of the car he turned, raised his arm and said politely, "Heil Hitler." Outside the windows the station master blew his whistle and the train went on into Germany.

PART TWO

A DEATH IN BOSTON

After the doctor had left, the medication was stopped and for the first time in more days than she could remember her mind was clear. But her body, all weakness and random pain, was something alien to her, a stick figure under the bedspread and the sheet.

She gathered her memories together and in her mind felt almost well again. She remembered the sun-filled days on the North Shore, and Grandfather arriving each evening from Boston. Potter would meet the train at Prides Crossing station, but Grandfather would take the reins himself and drive at a smart trot the leafy mile to the great house on the shore.

Strange that her memories were of Grandfather, and hardly at all of Father, who with the best will in the world had wasted the fortune and sold off the house at Prides and the town house on Beacon Street. Shamed by sudden poverty, she had taken an office job made for her by Grandfather's friends, and had toiled out a dim life on the edge of the world of her childhood. She lived on Beacon Street, but in a rooming house, where her raffish fellow tenants gave her willing respect and told their friends, quite accurately, that she was a Mayflower descendant.

She stirred in the bed, and tried to turn on her right side. The nurse's aide who came and went helped her to straighten out comfortably, and held a glass of water to her lips.

"I am going to die," she said, and the nurse's aide said, "What gave you that idea? What would you go and die for? Put that out of your mind."

"Am I dirty?," she asked, and the nurse's aide lifted the sheet and said, "Don't you worry about that. I'll fix you up in a jiffy, dear."

And she quickly washed her, and rolled her to one side of the bed and then the other as she changed the sheets. She put a fresh johnnie on her. "Try to think of pleasant things," she said.

Alone again, the old lady tried to find herself in the universe. Pleasant things. She named off the battle roll of her ancestors. There were gravestones with her family name on them at Burial Hill in Plymouth. There were sergeants and cornets in the Revolution, and an ancestor had been breveted colonel after the debacle of Fredericksburg.

"Dirty and dying," she said aloud, and repeated it like a child's nonsense verse. "Dirty and dying, dirty and dying."

The nurse's aide came in again and said, "You must try to sleep, dear."

"I am going to die," the old lady said.

"Nonsense," the nurse's aide said. "Now, haven't you told me that before?"

She was an attractive girl, slight but strong, with woven ropes of blond hair gathered under her white cap. She resembled the upstairs maid at Prides who had lulled a child to sleep, half-humming, half-singing. Often when the child had dropped to sleep, Grandfather would come up, smelling of port and cigars, and wake her to give him a goodnight kiss.

Pleasant things. All she could remember was lists. An old cotillion card with its list of dances: polka, waltz, schottische, Portland fancy. The wooden plaques Grandfather had nailed up in the garage, each bearing the name of an automobile he had owned: Stevens-Duryea, Mercer, Duesenberg, Marmon, Buick, Packard. The panel wagon from Pierce's rattling up to the kitchen door on Saturday afternoons, with cook standing in the white-tiled kitchen as Pierce's boy piled the groceries on the table.

Now, starting from her yellowed soles the cold was rising up her legs. It was like going into the surf in the early morning at Prides,

when the water numbed her as she walked in deeper and struck out with firm strokes. Then the cold, intimate touch of the sea was all over her body.

At last she knew that the rubric of death summoned her. She tried to remember the prayers Reverend Tolliver had given out as they knelt with bowed heads in the upholstered pew, a moment before Grandfather, in his white linen suit, had walked to the winged lectern to read something incomprehensible from St. Paul.

She remembered the Lord's Prayer, and then as the cold shook her she cried out to the Lord approaching her through the mist, walking on the water. "Well, Lord Jesus, I guess if You want me You'll have to take me as I am."

In the sleepy morning the nurse's aide came up to the lamp-lit desk where the day nurse was reading charts. The day nurse was a solid woman of forty, with thin yellow hair under a cap that rode on her head like a gauze cupcake.

"The poor thing is gone," the nurse's aide said. "We didn't expect her to last the night."

"When did that happen?" the day nurse said.

"Just now, I guess."

The day nurse picked up a stethoscope from the desk and went down the corridor for a few minutes, and then returned. She selected a steel-covered chart from the rack and wrote something in it.

"Shall I wash her up?" the nurse's aide said.

"Don't touch her," the day nurse said. "Don't touch anything until the doctor comes and pronounces her."

"She has a nephew who visited her some weeks ago. He wanted to be notified when she took a turn for the worse," the nurse's aide said.

"Oh, he was notified," the day nurse said.

"Too bad he didn't get here before she died," the nurse's aide said.

"I don't think that will bother him much," the day nurse said.

THE LISTENER

Mrs. Dowson stood in the doorway of Arthur's room and buttoned the cuff of her pink blouse. There had been a button missing but Marie had replaced it. She had found the same kind of button, a shiny pearl disk with four holes, and had sewed it on expertly, the thread criss-crossing under the fabric and not on the top of the button.

It wasn't really Marie's job. Lord knows she had enough to do, what with ordering the groceries from Sage's, cooking, setting the table, and lifting the metal trays into the dishwasher. That and getting Mrs. Deems, the cleaning woman, to do at least some vacuuming between the recitals of failed husbands, miscarriages, rising prices at the supermarket, and the rascality of politicians. Marie was a treasure, an old phrase Mrs. Dowson's mother had used to describe cooks who worked hard for low wages and never took home steaks in their satchels.

"Marie is a treasure," Mrs. Dowson said. "I don't know what I'd do without her. It's funny, my eyes are perfect, but the one thing I can't do is thread a needle. It must be eye-strain from doing too many crossword puzzles. I don't do embroidery any more, though I probably could if I put my mind to it."

She crossed Arthur's room to the mantel where a Seth Thomas clock stood over the brown-grained marble fireplace. It was stopped at two o'clock. Mrs. Dowson opened the glass front of the dial and set the hour to five minutes after nine, to match the hands on her baguette watch. She lifted the corner of the oaken clock and set the pendulum swinging, a gold wafer catching the light. It was lost effort. The brass key which should have been under the clock was missing.

"I hope you slept well, Arthur," Mrs. Dowson said. "Towards morning I had to put on a light blanket, and I turned on the radio and listened to some foolish talk show. People were telephoning in and asking questions about flying objects. It was an hour before I got to sleep again."

She sat in a tapestried armchair near the mantel, and smoothed her oyster linen skirt over her knees. Through the open window there was a sound of lawn-mowing. Beside the house a half-acre of lawn extended to a row of Lombardy poplars. There had been tennis courts there until Arthur had grassed them over. Near the house, in the shadow of a wineglass elm, there were a white table and white wooden chairs with cretonne cushions, under a tilted blue umbrella.

A boy on the saddle of the lawn mower, his naked back glistening with sweat, drove the mower down to the poplars and back to the house. Another boy, in cut-off jeans, stood on a step-ladder and trimmed flat the top of the yew hedge. As the mower passed the hedge the boys exchanged genial abuse over the clatter of the blades.

"The days are longer," Mrs. Dowson said. "You know I like to get up with the sun, but five-thirty is too early. But how lovely to hear the first bird! Yesterday I timed the first one—a robin, I think—and it was nine minutes past four. Don't you think there are more birds this year? They say that since people have stopped using all those insecticides, the birds are coming back. I suppose we can thank Rachel Carson for that.

"Marie says the same oven birds that were here last year have nested in the elm. How can she be sure they are the same ones? There were some new birds at the birdbath yesterday. I should look them up in your bird book. Grosbeaks, I think. And there were gulls, dozens of them, flying in to Batton's Pond. They say gulls like to wash their feathers in fresh water.

"You remember the gulls at Boothbay and how they would fly over a rock and drop clams to break the shells? What clever creatures they are! And all at once the whole crowd of gulls would

54

fly off to meet a fishing boat coming back to the harbor. Strange that they would know which boat was gutting fish and which wasn't.

"I used to wish you weren't such an avid fisherman, going out each day in Cahoon's boat, even on days when the weather was so bad that the natives stayed on shore. It was lonely sometimes. Sometimes the other women would josh me and say that they were golf widows, but I was a fishing widow."

Suddenly she began to weep, the sobs rising from her chest and making her catch her breath. She took a blue handkerchief from the pocket of her skirt and covered her face. "I saw even less of you at home," she said. "It wasn't just the fishing, Arthur. It was anything that attracted you, anything at all.

"No more tears, Arthur," she said, at last, as she replaced the handkerchief in her pocket. "You don't like tears and I've tried never to annoy you. But how long will I wait for a reply? You are being cruel to me, though you are not a cruel man. But the world is cruel. Men do as they please and get away with it. But once when I was lonely, I fell. Only once, with someone who meant nothing to me except that he was gentle, and noticed my coloring and my hair, and touched my face. And he was here. He was here, Arthur, and God knows where you were, for days at a time.

"I atoned. I know God has forgiven me because God is good. But you never did. It hurt your pride. I was one of your possessions that someone had used. I don't blame you,—but Arthur, how long will you make me wait for a word? One word?"

From the hall, up the echo chamber of the stairs, the D-toned bell of the grandfather clock struck ten. Mrs. Dowson dabbed once more at her eyes, went into her room and put on a grey top-coat. She spoke to Marie in the kitchen and then went out the pillared door and down the flagstoned walk. Potter was waiting with the blue Lincoln.

As they drove through the pylons at the gate of Mount Auburn Cemetery she spoke to Potter for the first time, now as she always did. The flowers and lawns were beautifully kept, she said.

Oh—there were pink begonias in the circular flower bed over Mary Baker Eddy's tomb. The forsythia were gone by, but the spirea, "bridal veil," were coming into flower.

They passed the graves she knew, and she spoke the names aloud as she saw the granite blocks and limestone urns and gesturing statues: Longfellow, Amy Lowell, Francis Parkman, Edwin Booth, Winslow Homer. They were her neighbors now, however life had exalted them and set them apart.

At Tulip Path, Potter stopped the Lincoln at the grass verge, and came around to open the door for her. Like a verger he went ahead of her, an old man in a chauffeur's black uniform. They went up the grassy lane, by the oblong bulk of brownstone dedicated to Nathaniel Bowditch, the Salem clerk whose marvelous book, crammed with pilots' lore and tables of logarithms, had brought the ships of the nineteenth century into port.

On Orchis Path, Potter stopped at a small mausoleum, its grey blocks of Quincy granite fitted together like pieces of fondant. The brass door opened easily to the key and disclosed a narrow space lit by a small stained glass window of Connick blue, with a red angel displaying a Latin promise from St. Paul.

The chauffeur took yesterday's roses from the shelf over the marble sarcophagus, and replaced them with a sheaf of yellow azaleas. Then he went down the path, and sat in the car.

Mrs. Dowson seated herself in the metal armchair, drew off her gloves and folded them in her lap.

"Good morning, Arthur," she said. "I am here."

A DOG WITH NO SENSE

The phone rang sharply at the end of the bar. Jim wiped his hands on the red and white checked towel over the sink and went down to the wall phone.

"Yeah?" he asked, holding the receiver between his shoulder and his ear. He looked at his right hand, and took the fingernail of his little finger between his teeth.

"Jim." There was the sound of a caught breath and a woman sobbing. "Jim, Jonas has been run over. He's out on the sidewalk and he can't walk. His hind legs—"

"What was he doing out there?" Jim asked. "Marie, I told you not to let him out by himself. Never mind. I'm sorry."

"Jim, the vet is here. He says Jonas has no chance. His hind legs are crushed." She sobbed again. "He wants to give him the needle."

"No," Jim said, "don't let him kill that dog." He glanced down along the bar to where Schultzie, the proprietor, seated at the angle of the bar, was going through some bills. Inside the bar, the kid, in a white apron and a white paper cap, was putting sandwiches in the glass case.

"I'll be right over," Jim said, and hung up.

"Schultzie," he said, "my dog has been hit by a car. I've got to get over there. I'll be only half an hour?"

"Okay," Schultzie said. He took his glasses off, lifting the wire bow from each ear, and looked at the railroad clock over the bottles. Its hands showed 11:10. "Be back by twelve, okay?"

"No sweat," Jim said. He took off the red jacket and hung it at the end of the bar beside the phone.

Schultzie sighed, gathered up the bills and came down the length of the bar. He put on a jacket as Jim went out the side door to the parking lot. At twelve the hard hats from the construction job down the street would be in for a sandwich and beer. And the alcoholics from the nearby offices would show up for their noon-day rations.

"It's the dog," Schultzie said to the kid and to the three patrons who hunched over their drinks. "Last week his wife called; she's sick. He tells her to take a Valium and lie down. Now, becoss the dog gets clipped on the street, he goes out of here like his butt was on fire."

One of the drinkers went over to the Wurlitzer, twirled the selector and inserted a quarter. The machine clicked and then gave out a waltz, all sugary saxophones and a heavy beat.

"You're wrong about Jim and the dog," the kid said, looking at the polished wood of the bar.

"How would you know?" Schultzie asked. The music dipped and soared.

"I listen to him," the kid said.

There was a police car in front of the house. One officer was at the wheel listening to the chatter of the police radio; his partner was standing on the sidewalk with a few neighbors: three women and some children. Marie, in a blue bathrobe and open-toed slip-pers, was talking to the vet, a short man in a brown suit with two pens clipped into a vest pocket. A thin arrow of hair divided the shining skin of his head.

"A neighbor called Emergency," the policeman said. "The dog was in the street trying to crawl. The neighbor said a green station wagon hit him, and didn't stop."

Jim turned on Marie and said, "Who sent for the vet? Is he another one of your friends?"

His wife covered her mouth with her hand. "Oh, Jim," she almost whispered, "you're so suspicious. There's nothing..."

"I'm a professional man," the vet said. "I don't need to take that from you."

"We called him," the officer said. "Regulations. We can't shoot a dog or a skunk or a lion loose from the zoo."

"Jim," Marie said, "Jonas is all through. You've got to put him out of his misery."

Jim knelt beside the dog, who was lying at their feet, his hind legs stretched out, the yellow fur bloodied. A brown leather strap held his jaws together. Jim took the dog's head on his knee and touched the strap. The dog's eyes opened and he growled and whined, and jerked his head towards his left shoulder.

"Who put that thing on him?" Jim said.

"I did," the vet said. "He'll bite anything." The dog rolled his eyes towards Jim, and foam came to his lips.

"Do you want me to put him to sleep or not?" the vet said. "I can't stay here all day."

"He's a thoroughbred," Jim said. "A good collie is hard to get. We have the papers." He stroked the dog's long Hapsburg nose.

"He must be in a helluva lot of pain," the policeman said. "There's nothing you can do."

Jim stood up and rubbed his chin in a motion down from his right ear. The dog growled in his chest, and jerked his head from side to side.

"Okay," Jim said. The policeman motioned the people back, and the vet went for the hypodermic in his black bag.

Jim was back at the bar at three minutes to twelve. All the stools were taken, but the big crowd, who would line up behind the stools and take their drinks and sandwiches standing, had not arrived. Jim worked steadily until two o'clock with Schultzie and the kid, serving drinks with the graceful motions built into his arm muscles, keeping the bar clean, responding without small talk to a request made by a murmur or a nod or a finger touching a glass. He was good and he knew it.

When there were only a dozen customers left, the leisurely after-noon drinkers, Schultzie said, "Jim, what happened to the dog?"

"Someone in a green station wagon hit him and kept on going. We had to let the vet give him the needle. He's only three months old and couldn't go out by himself, but my wife let him out a few times and he stayed behind the house. Today he dashed out into the street, and the station wagon ran over him."

"Tough to lose a dog," Schultzie said. "Two years ago I lost a German shepherd, black with silver paws? We fed him good, okay, but he always raided garbage around the neighborhood. Some dogs are regular scavengers, you know? He ate something that poisoned him. That dog cost me two hundred dollars."

"Jonas cost me three," Jim said. "My wife always wanted a dog, a collie like she had when she was a kid. We got him at a kennel in Winchester, with kennel club papers, and he was registered, you know? My wife would talk to the dog, and take him shopping, and he was a real companion for her. You save what you can. But she shouldn't have let him out of her sight."

"He was too young of a dog," Schultzie agreed.

"He was too young," Jim said. "He was a dog with no sense."

LANDSCAPE

When the phone rang Mr. Blaisdell took off his glasses, turned down the noise of the television, and went out to the hall.

"Yes?" he said.

"Will you accept a collect call from Carl Smith?"

"Who?" Mr. Blaisdell's eyes shifted. "Oh, yes; I'll take it."

"Dad? You weren't supposed to accept the call. Don't you remember the code? How are you?"

"Well, I'm feeling first-rate. I'm not training for the Olympics, but I'm fine. Is everything all right?"

"A call from Carl Smith is supposed to mean that I've reached Des Moines, o.k. I didn't want to lay a collect call on you."

"Well, your mother remembers the signals. I don't. Who will you be in Omaha?"

"Dad, everything's going o.k., except Donna was sick in Cleveland."

"What was the matter with her?"

"Some kind of ear infection. I had to use a chunk of the cash I have. The doctor wouldn't take a credit card."

"Why didn't she call her family? You're not responsible for her. Her father must own half of Norfolk County. He could have flown out a doctor from the Eye and Ear. He probably owns that, too."

"Always the comedian. Is mom o.k.?"

"She's fine. She'll be disappointed not to talk with you. She's out at some meeting about ecology. I have the most social-minded family, and no one's ever at home."

"Give her my love, dad."

"She misses you. She keeps expecting you to walk in the door."

ONCE UPON A TIME

Her presence is all through the house. As you enter the hallway with its model T phone on a small table, you look into the living room across a varnished wooden gate. You push a button in the top of the gate, and Rose Kennedy's recorded voice says, "Welcome to our home."

She points out the red armchair where Joseph P. Kennedy sat in the evening reading *The Boston Transcript.* Rose darned stockings, or sat at the grand piano that was the wedding gift of her uncles. Jack and his older brother Joe played with their building blocks on the oriental carpet until bedtime.

Then Rose and Joseph Kennedy would take long walks through the streets of Brookline, down Beals Street from the green clapboard house, along Abbotsford Road, to which they would move when the family got larger, past St. Aidan's Church on Freeman Street, where the children were baptized and where Joe and Jack would be altar boys.

There are three rooms on the first floor of 83 Beals Street: the living room, the dining room, and the kitchen. Joseph and Rose Kennedy moved into the heavily mortgaged house after their marriage in 1914. Cardinal O'Connell had married them in the chapel of his residence. Kennedy was president of the Columbia Trust Company, the youngest bank president in the country. Rose was the daughter of John F. Fitzgerald, a former mayor of Boston.

The dining room is set for dinner, with the Limoges porcelain and the children's napkin rings, and the teacups that were the appropriate gift of Sir Thomas Lipton. The kitchen is a period piece, with a coal range and a coal hod and a beanpot; a washboard and a cake of bon-ami soap. At the kitchen table the cook and the nursemaid who slept in the dormered attic took their meals.

Upstairs in the nine-room house, in a little study, Rose wrote her letters and kept a file box with the records of the children's milestones and illnesses: confirmation and first communion, weekly weight, whooping cough and chicken pox, and Jack's scarlet fever. On the walls over the stairwell are framed pictures of peewee football squads: Jack playing for Dexter School, Joe and Jack for Lower Noble School.

In the master bedroom are twin beds with white spreads and plain brown walnut headboards, and an array of baby pictures (the six-month pictures) on the wall. Here Dr. Frederick L. Good delivered the second child. Rose Kennedy's voice breaks the stillness: "The President was born in the twin bed near the window on May 29, 1917, at 3 o'clock in the afternoon."

Then, "Every mother can influence her son to a great extent...And what you do with him and for him has influence, not for a day or for a year, but for time and eternity."

The house has been a National Historic Site since 1967. Six years before, the town of Brookline had erected a bronze plaque set in granite in the tiny front yard.

Visitors number over 30,000 a year, but this year the number is running considerably higher. Japanese tourists visit the house in large numbers. Mrs. S. Yatsuhashi, as a young wife living a few houses away, at 66 Beals Street, remembers Rose wheeling Joe and Jack in a baby carriage. On the front porch Jack rode his kiddie car—an elf-like creature of two years in a starched white sailor suit.

In the nursery, with its little white-counterpaned bed and bassinet, Joe and Jack slept during their first year or so, until Rosemary was born. On a clothestree hang the long christening gown and bonnet, of white silk and lace, that all the Kennedy children wore, and later John Jr., at baptism. There is a toy railroad with two khaki-colored coaches and a locomotive. On a low stool near the door is one of Jack's favorite books, *King Arthur and His Knights.*

Douglas Sabin, the National Park System official in charge, remarks on the reverential air of the visitors who throng the house in these spring days when the forsythia are golden on Beals Street and the sycamore in leaf. "Many, when they leave the nursery," Sabin says, "are quite visibly moved."

I know.

ANTHEMS

I am an enthusiastic singer of national anthems. Possessed—I am not going to change that word—possessed of a sturdy baritone which some have found too self-indulgent but in which the more thoughtful have recognized a Cremona timbre, I have borne my gift through the heedless marketplace.

As a freshman at Holy Cross, I tried out for the glee club and was rejected. I report this fact, which my friends find hard to credit, without rancor. Others who applied at the same time, some under the impression that they were trying out for working beagles on the Myopia Hunt, were accepted. I was reduced by nameless prejudice to singing in boisterous quartets and despairing church choirs, even to competing with the bell-ringers on Beacon Hill on Christmas Eve.

My private sorrow has not burked my pleasure at joining in national anthems. I remember Coronation Day in 1953 when hundreds of well-wishers crowded Symphony Hall to watch a review of a hastily assembled company of veterans of the Queen's service parading in the beautiful slow march. Then we heard Her Majesty speaking from overseas to "my people," and responded by lifting the coffered ceiling with "God Save the Queen," and, for good measure, "The Maple Leaf Forever."

I remember Lily Pons, like a girl from Domremy on a white horse, singing the "*Marseillaise*" in Rockefeller Plaza the day Paris was liberated. I was in the new Abbey Theatre for its opening in July, 1966, and sang to all the suffering and glory that had made Ireland a nation again. That was "The Soldier's Song" (rather wide-ranging for the voice, and rough terrain for the bagpipes):

"Soldiers are we whose lives are pledged to Ireland;

Some have come from a land across the wave."

Indeed we had; half the audience were Americans.

I remember when Pope Paul VI made his fourteen-hour visit to New York to preach, like Paul on the Areopagus, to the General Assembly of the United Nations. It was an incredibly crowded day, climaxed with a moving liturgy in Yankee Standium. For Catholics of the old school and the old parish, like myself, it was a time as historic as the naming of a new planet. It seemed to bring America's infinity of neighborhoods together, to make us one fold for an hour, knowing one shepherd.

When, before his departure, he had circled the stadium with arms lifted to the crowd, and the Dunwoodie Seminary choir had sung "Now Thank We All Our God," and Archbishop Sheen, announcing for television, had said with pardonable sentimentality, "Good night, sweet Prince,"— then the choir did a stunning thing. They sang "The Star-Spangled Banner."

It was as if they were saying thanks to the great Pope who had called the world to a higher cubit of dignity. No more feuds between the nations. No more plundering of colonies for gold and copper and oil. No more bullying the weak and enforcing honor by mallard-fleets of bombers staining the sky. "If you wish to be brothers, let the weapons fall from your hands...No more war, war never again!"

Peace was no longer a pedantic illusion but a future we could plan for, as a man plans security and education for his children. So the creaky old patriotic words of the song rang like a carillon, and we thought what a dawn it indeed was, and how that early light would enlarge and flood like the morning of the world. That was Oct. 4, 1965.

Oh, my country! I cannot sing your anthem now.

1973

ON GETTING INTO WHO'S WHO

Having recently seen my name and short and simple annals included in the new edition (the 38th) of *Who's Who in America*, I was attracted by a sentence I just read in one of the admirable books of E. B. White. "A great many of the most indolent characters in the United States," White wrote, "are listed in *Who's Who*."

This is cheering news, for I had wondered what sort of unwonted effort or knightly leadership would be required of me.

This is not the first time I had been listed in domesday books. Some years ago I was named to the Gallery of Living Catholic Authors, and was asked to send a photograph and some pages of manuscript, presumably to be filed in the library of a midwestern college.

I haven't heard from the Gallery for some time, and have wondered whether it had been abandoned or whether I was thought to have given up the Faith, authorship, or life: all greatly exaggerated.

There is a kind of publishing venture known as a "mug book." Some of them have honored me beyond my deserts. A mug book is a listing of short biographies, some of them with photographs, of as many people as the publisher can cram into a closely-printed volume. The biographees are at liberty to purchase a copy: the latest example was offered to me for $34.50, or two for $50.

One of these, a book called something like *Social Leaders and Great Citizens*, informed me that after careful screening and on the recommendations of other social leaders and great citizens, I had been selected for inclusion. Such was the confidence the editors had in me that I was asked to suggest other social leaders who might be listed, or mugged.

Some of these thoughts, sardonic and self-deflating, were in my mind when I went back to Holy Cross for a mid-winter visit. The college was on vacation when I walked up that impossible hillside the Nipmucks called the Hill of Pleasant Springs, Pakachoag. I indulged the harmless melancholy of a return to times past as I prowled the empty campus and admired again the beauty and order of the Georgian buildings.

Here was lordly Fenwick, with its white Corinthian columns and dormer windows, the granite foundation still scarred from the fire of 1852.

Here was Dinand Library, a Roman temple with a flourish of scripture on its architrave, at the top of a "Niagara of granite,"—Dinand Steps. Next to it, in a covert of trees, is small, red-brick Beaven Hall, "heavenly Beaven," the dorm where I lived in junior year, the happiest year of my life.

Beyond Fenwick, a privet hedge enclosed the college cemetery, with the long ranks of the minimal headstones of Jesuits. In the oldest corner is the more ornate monument of the founder, Bishop Benedict Joseph Fenwick. The flowery inscription is in Latin, with a translation on the back of the stone for those whose Latin, like John Courtney Murray's Bulgarian, is rusty.

I looked about me, down to the sluggish Blackstone River, up the crowded hill, at the landscape of Holy Cross— so old and so new and changed. I remembered the words of Michael Earls '96:

> Mother, be thy colors
> Royal in our care;
> Time, that makes men older,
> Finds thee young and fair.

I entered the college chapel, with its rather narrow facade but its interior a rising harmony of spaces. The white barrel vault with its hexagonal coffering leads to a stone apse that is strangely moving in its severity. Four columns of red polished granite uphold the golden baldachino like a crown held over a king's head at a coronation.

Through the lovely glass the winter sun made pools of color on the marble pavement; the martyrs' windows are set in the north wall, confessors' in the south.

At the west end of the chapel, between the three doors, are two oak tablets headed with the arms of the United States and of Holy Cross. Here are carved the names of alumni who died in two wars. The victims of earlier battles, the Union and Confederate dead, are recorded elsewhere.

I read all the names, musing on how death had met each one. Did it come to them in a detonating moment, or was there time for thoughts of home and of what arms had been around them and what hearts would cry out at the terrible news?

Did they think of spring evenings at Holy Cross with guitars and voices sounding in the quadrangles? And the lights going out, window by window, as the curfew bell rang from its creaky Fenwick turret?

There were nine men of the Class of 1939 who never came to any reunion. All of them I knew; four of them were my friends. Here they are, the names copied from an oaken tablet in an empty chapel filled with voices: Chester A. Bassett, Robert C. Gavin, David J. Murphy, Donald F. O'Sullivan, Louis J. Rylisko, Charles E. Smith, William E. Sullivan, William P. Sullivan, Francis E. Thorton, Jr.

What am I and what have I done to compare with who they were and what they gave?

BE SWIFT, MY SOUL

It is a melancholy experience for those who live, as I do, on the edge of a great city, or who travel through small towns, to see loitering in the shops and public squares, or entering squalid tenements on dingy streets, a multitude of human beings who have lived beyond their time. These unfortunates, instead of being able to work for their honest livelihood, are condemned to live on public charity or to survive on pensions that scarcely buy food and warmth, in a time of soaring prices, or furnish shelter at a time when landlords must continually raise their rents.

I think that all parties will agree that this alarming number of the elderly, living at the grudging welcome of their families or dwelling in little apartments in the gray horror of loneliness and increasing incompetence, presents a crisis no less grave than any that confronts our nation. Therefore, whoever could find a fair, cheap and easy method of solving this problem would merit everyone's thanks and deserve the honor accorded a benefactor of the republic.

Having several friends who fall into the melancholy category I have described, I have given considerable study to the problem over many years, and I have noted the shortsighted and indeed sentimental answers that society has so far provided. I urge, therefore, that we all confront the issue squarely.

There is a way out that not only will benefit the republic in a time of financial straits and of natural resources once prodigal but now grown parsimonious, but also will prevent any resort on the part of the young and the vigorous middle-aged to taking matters into their own hands, disposing of their unwanted elderly at private venture or leaving them to starve or freeze.

I propose to provide for the unwanted elderly in a manner that will free them from the tedious serving out of existence in a backwater of life, distressing to their descendants and to themselves. Let us all have the absolute right (or let the state exercise it for us), guaranteed by legislation and reaffirmed by our enlightened courts, to procure the death of our unwanted elderly citizens at the age of seventy years.

Exceptions, of course, may be allowed: families who treasure a grandparent as a focus of family affection, or as a source of income, or as a baby sitter; individuals whose usefulness whether in the public service, in medicine, in the arts or in commerce belies their advanced years. These might legitimately plead exemption. But I would stress the warning that sentimentality and outworn forms of civility might here impair the common good. And I would urge that such instances be truly regarded as exceptions. The touchstone in this matter should always be the word "unwanted," and, if that clear criterion is met, the general rule should prevail.

Clinics should be established in which life may be terminated after simple forms are filled out to record that the elderly person (or senior citizen) is certainly unwanted. (This determination will be all the easier in the case of those who have outlived all their relatives and friends.) *Let no one imagine that technicians will be lacking to staff these humane facilities.*

I can foresee several solid benefits that will follow if this proposal is accepted. There would be a general exodus from our nursing homes and from the chronic illness wards of our hospitals. The tax structure, burdened by the support of the poor and the unwanted, would be greatly strengthened. The young and the vigorous middle-aged would enjoy a new *Lebensraum* consequent on the weeding-out of those made unfit by age for congenial social intercourse. All men and women troubled by the uncertainty of life would be reassured, at least, that the law would end it for them at seventy years.

A very worthy person, a true lover of his country, has recently suggested that the problem of the aged and the unwanted be settled within the family, or by some tacit arrangement apart from the remedy of statute law. But, with due deference to so deserving a patriot, I cannot be altogether of his sentiment. Who does not know of regrettable instances where citizens, impatient at the slow decline of their unwanted relatives, have had to enlist the help of unsavory characters employing brutal and unsanitary means? Who has not heard of a young woman, desperate at the unexpected longevity of a grandmother, who strangled this unwanted elder citizen with a coat hanger?

I pass over as unworthy of debate any objection based on an assumed sancitity of human life, or on the now archaic oath sworn by doctors since flames blazed on Apollo's altar. I reject the typically emotional and irrelevant plea that the law extend to every segment of human life the protection it affords to sea gulls.

Nor shall I dwell on the idle speculation that the use of the criterion "unwanted," which today may condemn the old, will tomorrow condemn the insane, the retarded or the eccentric, and next week the Gypsies, the Jews, the Slavs and Jehovah's Witnesses, the Catholics, the politically intransigent... But here I digress, and my mind has wandered to another nation's history, not our own.

GIFT OF THE MAGI

When the two elderly women came into the waiting room, the nurse at the desk couldn't tell, at first, which was the patient. Then she saw one guiding the other to a chair. The blind woman, helpless in a strange place, nevertheless sat with a dignity that recalled the repose of ancient statuary.

The sighted woman approached the desk and said, "My mother..." and the nurse rose and moved another chair to the side of the desk. She seated both women and began to fill out a file card. The daughter answered the questions except for a few, like the place of birth and the year, when the mother responded. She was 104 years old.

When the doctor was ready they walked into his consulting room. He read the older woman's name and asked her nationality. She was voluble and smiling after the doctor, remembering the speech of his grandparents, spoke to her in her own tongue.

"Doctor, I am 104 now and I do not have my sight for over twenty years. All my life I have never been sick, never sick enough to bother the doctor, except when the children came.

"Doctor, I have a happy life. When my eyes began to grow dark and I couldn't read the paper even with the big glass, I accept this as part of growing old. Doctor, I have such good children. I remember all their faces and can speak to them and touch them. I am not a burden. I take care of myself. I know how lucky I am to have such a family.

"But, doctor, lately I am sad." She seemed embarrassed to go on, like a child afraid to make a foolish request. "Doctor, I have five great-grandchildren I have never seen."

The doctor turned on the bright overhead light and looked through an instrument a long time into each eye. As he helped her out of the big metal chair she said apologetically, "Doctor, if you can give my eyes six hours of sight to see my great-grandchildren, I die happy."

"I think," the doctor said in a steady voice, "I think we may be able to do better than that."

She entered the hospital on a Thursday afternoon and early Friday the doctor operated. Afterwards she lay waiting, accustomed to darkness, responding to the voices beside her and to the hands that lifted her and tipped liquids into her mouth. No; no pain.

On Sunday morning the doctor removed the bandages and tested her sight and fitted thick-lensed temporary glasses. For a quiet time she enjoyed the color of light and how it touched the yellow walls and the white bed and the waving green of a tree outside the window.

Then the corridor was alive with sound: voices and laughter and the questions of children. They crowded into the room, children and grandchildren, strangers for a moment and then familiar. The five great-grandchildren stood around her, and one of them lifted the youngest up into her arms.

Child by child they told her the names she knew.

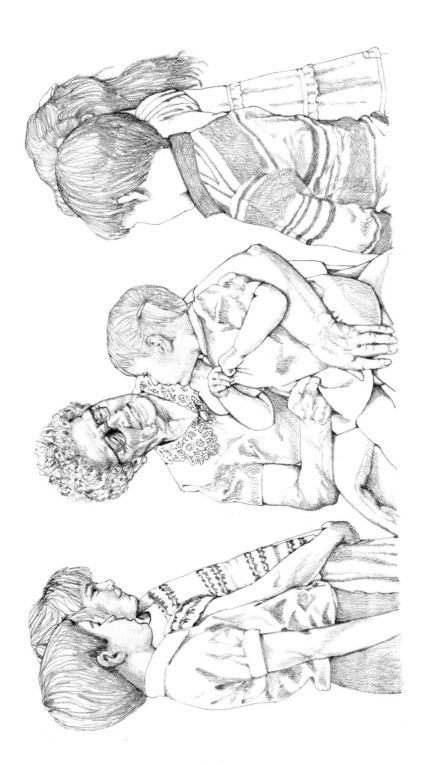

BOSTON TO ME

Boston to me is the poetry of its street names: Cornhill, Cricket Lane, Haymarket, Pudding Lane, Appian Way, Province Steps, Batterymarch, Damnation Alley, Pie Alley, Turnagain Alley, Winter Street, Summer, Autumn, Spring.

Boston is the "crooked but interesting" streets themselves that wind not so much to follow cow paths but to amble around a pump or a lost brook or an immemorial tree.

Boston is Boston Common, "a pasture for cows, a playground for children, a place for beating carpets, a training ground for the militia."

Boston is the Athenaeum ghost, and the grave of Mrs. Mary Goose in the Old Granary.

Boston is Mr. Paul Revere's State House dome shining through the trees like the crock of gold.

Boston is the Common trees labeled by their Latin botanical names, with a translation for visitors.

Boston is the Common pigeons, tough as boatswains, and a thousand sparrows twittering at nightfall on the facade of one building.

Boston is a stenographer lying in the noon sun on the bank of the Public Garden pond, reading Immanuel Kant.

Boston is the carillon of Brimstone Corner sprinkling ponderous joy on the noontime air.

Boston is the Old State House where America was hammered out on the anvil of the Boston Town Meeting.

Boston is Durgin Park Market Dining Room, and its indomitable waitresses dishing out Yankee rations of clam chowder, poor man's roast beef, apple pan dowdy, Indian pudding.

Boston is a jubilant wedding in the North End with the bride showered with Jordan almonds, a custom as old as Vergil's *Georgics*.

Boston is King Louis Philippe teaching French in a garret at 41 Union Street.

Boston is *Godspell*, and Summerthing and Winterfest and midsummer music on the Charles.

Boston is Robert Gould Shaw and his black regiment marching in St. Gaudens' incomparable bronze.

Boston is Bartholdi's trumpeting angels on the tower of First Baptist, the "Church of the Holy Beanblowers."

Boston is the gleaming ranks of the Sargents at the Museum of Fine Arts, and Monet's water lilies, and thin-lipped Stuarts, and the proudest aristocrat in Boston—the Minoan goddess in gold and ivory, 3,500 years old.

Boston is the young Robert Frost spending his money at the Old Corner Book Store, and walking home to Lawrence.

Boston is T.S. Eliot taking boxing lessons at a gymnasium in the South End.

Boston is Old Ironsides with the blue flag of the fleet still flying at her mainmast.

Boston is Rowes Wharf and Long Wharf, and India Wharf and T Wharf and Constitution Wharf and Battery Wharf and Griffin's Wharf, North Ferry and South Ferry, and the bittersweet memory of streets ending in a thicket of masts.

Boston is Sarah Caldwell, a moment before the overture begins, lifting her baton like Zeus gathering thunderbolts.

Boston is Jack Kennedy saying, "I'm glad to be back where words are pronounced as they are spelled."

Boston is the prayer graven on her shield: "As God was with our Founders, so may He be with us."

JOE NAGLE

Joe Nagle is a short, thin, intense man with a pointed chin and a short neck. His shirt collars reach to just below his ears, which gives him the appearance of disappearing into his clothes.

He works regularly as a messenger for a Boston bank, and in the evenings he goes to wakes whether he knows the deceased or not. He claims to be a very sick man in a miscellaneous way, and by reading anatomy textbooks, memoirs of surgeons, medical journals, and ancient collections of quack remedies, he has acquired considerable confidence in identifying and predicting diseases. He has a supreme contempt for doctors. "They take your money," he said recently, "and what do they do for you? Nothing, nothing *nothing*."

He goes to wakes to inquire of the survivors what the deceased person died of, and to suggest that the medical attention was inadequate. Or he launches into a long description of his own ailments, with the intention of cheering up the bereaved relatives by the knowledge that other people have troubles too. When they are planning to visit a funeral home, people will sometimes ask, "Has Joe Nagle been there yet?"

One tactful undertaker suggested to Joe that he make his visit early on the first night. Joe accepted this as a tribute to his powers of consoling, and tried to follow out the suggestion. The undertaker might have saved his breath. Nagle, once he has hurried into the wake house with the zest of the old firehorse smelling the burning orphanage, is inclined to stay on.

There is a story which I am unable to verify that Mr. Nagle was once forbidden entrance to a Lithuanian funeral home in South Boston by the undertaker, on the grounds that the client's family had suffered enough.

His background is rather vague, and subject to revision. He seems to have been born in Providence, Rhode Island, and to have attended Dartmouth College sometime in the presidency of Warren G. Harding. He majored in Latin, and may have completed the sophomore year.

"At the end of my second year at Dartmouth College, Hanover, New Hampshire," Mr. Nagle once said, "a traveling caricaturist gave a demonstration and immediately I knew what I wanted to be. I kissed Horace and Tacitus goodbye and haven't looked them up since."

Before drifting into other pursuits he spent at least a year drawing lightning caricatures for the tourist trade on Fisherman's Wharf in San Francisco. When asked where he came from, he would say, "Boston, Mass. I used to pahk my cah on Pahk Street."

When I asked Mr. Nagle why he supplied this inaccurate item in his history, he said, "Because no one west of the Berkshires knows where in God's name Providence is. Boston, yes; Portland, Maine, yes. But Providence, no."

Though not a drinking man, Mr. Nagle goes on a bat of about ten days' duration once a year, and this seems to be overlooked at the bank. "Sick leave," Mr. Nagle said recently about one of these interludes. "I haven't had a well day in thirty years."

As a matter of fact, he seems to be in rude health; he says he has survived in spite of the worst efforts of the medical profession. "Food is the key to longevity," he once said. "No meat, no eggs, just cereal grains and fruit, fresh vegetables and nuts." He patronizes health food stores from which he buys alfalfa honey and rose hips, and figs and other fruits dried without preservatives.

At the end of one of his annual sick leaves I met him in Copley Square. His face was puffed and there was a bandage under his left eye. "Eight stitches," he said. "A young Pakistani doctor sewed me up over at the Charitable Eye and Ear. Charitable my foot! It cost me ten dollars—that's one dollar and twenty-five cents a stitch. They've got a goldmine over there."

He declined to explain how he had been wounded.

I met Mr. Nagle recently in George Gloss's second-hand bookstore on West Street. This is a marvelous rookery which resembles not so much a bookstore as a loft into which the contents of a bookstore have been moved after an air-raid.

I was picking my way out of the cluttered store when I saw Mr. Nagle standing alone in front of the wall cases, a book in his hand, reading aloud. It is a tribute to the freedom and humanity of George Gloss's establishment that no one seemed to think that this was strange.

Nagle greeted me warmly, keeping his left thumb in the book. "It's been months since we talked," he said. "Let's go over to Bailey's. I'll shout you to an ice cream soda."

Seated on metal chairs at a round, marble-topped table, we drank our ice-cream sodas and Mr. Nagle favored me with one of his stories of his conflicts with, and timely exposure of, the medical profession.

"I was young and innocent then," Mr. Nagle said, "before I knew what they were up to. I was limping in one leg and someone recommended Twitchell, the orthopedic man. When I went into his office I said, 'Doctor, I'm limping in one leg.' He said, 'Walk up and down there in front of the desk.' Well, I did that, limping in one leg.

"'You have uni-lateral claudication.' Twitchell said.

"'Doctor,' I replied, 'I knew that before I came in here. *I know as much Latin as you do.*'"

Mr. Nagle opened a newspaper on the table and ran his finger down the death column. "Tonight I'm going to pay my respects to the late Mortimer Gaffney. He's at Dooley's over to the Gate. Did you know Gaffney?" I said that I did not.

"A good, steady man, but he did have the failing in his younger days. He would come home on pay-night tight as a barn owl and

beat up his wife a little to show her who was boss.

"Well, she took it for a while, and then she had a word with Monsignor Corkery. Did you know Monsignor Corkery? A fine, gloomy man with the shoulders of a black Angus bull, who ran the parish like a barony. Shortly thereafter Monsignor Corkery happened to meet Mortimer when the day shift was getting out of the Edison.

" 'Mort,' he said, 'walk along with me for a moment. I hear you have been laying violent hands on your little wife. Do it once more, Mort, and I will meet you here, in front of the Edison, and break your nose.' It was a heavenly marriage from that time on."

I have the testimony of a reliable observer who was seated that night on a folding chair near the coffin of Mortimer Gaffney. There was a line down the steps out to Dorchester Street because Mrs. Gaffney is a high official in the Catholic Daughters.

Mr. Nagle arrived at the coffin in his turn, gave the widow a two-handed handshake, and began his words of condolence.

"My heartfelt sympathy, Mrs. Gaffney. You have lost a fine man who will be remembered for his honest and hard-working life. But misfortune comes to all of us; you today, me tomorrow. Today I got the bad news from the hospital. I had the blood test and the barium x-ray at the City last week. Today I had a nurse read the plates, and guess what I have? *Cyanosis of the small intestine.* The doctors are powerless."

Here Mr. Nagle executed a manoeuver which is customary with him. He stepped to the side of the widow and continued to talk to her while others moved up in line and offered their sympathy.

"The doctors are powerless," he continued. "I know what they are going to say: surgery. No, Mrs. Gaffney,—not me. Injections? No. Expensive anti-biotics or sulfa or any other nostrum from their medieval herbal books? No, I'm handling this myself. How, you ask? *By the water cure.*

"One of the unacknowledged medical wizards of the last century was a learned Dominican monk by the name of Father Kneipp. He rediscovered the natural curative powers of water. As

far back as you can trace, mankind has found the health he needed in baths. There were medicinal baths in Italy, there were baths
in France, there were baths in Germany. Our own American In-
dians used bathing as an effective cure.

"Am I going to Baden-Baden, Vichy, or Hot Springs? No, Mrs.
Gaffney, I am not. I'm remaining here in Boston, in my humble
home, and *spending seven hours a day in my own bathtub with the hot
water up to my chin.*"

At this point, two of the Gaffney relatives, young men in dark
suits with black ties, who had been glaring at Mr. Nagle, approached him and steered him away from the widow.

"Mrs. Gaffney," Mr. Nagle called back, "you know I'm sorry for
your trouble."

"I know you are," Mrs. Gaffney said.

A DEFENSE AGAINST GARDEN PESTS

If you want to know how things are in Chestnut Hill, I must report that they are just as bad as in any other suburb. People are tending vegetable gardens and telling you about them.

Once the snows of February disappear and the first foolhardy robin appears, small talk takes a bucolic turn. Improbable friendships blossom on the secret of where to buy the best tomato plants (invariably thirty miles away, but worth the trip).

I have seen some well known academic men, wearing their expensive educations like necromancer cloaks, spend the better part of an evening quarreling about cutworms.

There are some families, not otherwise lacking civic virtue and neighborly *gemuetlichkeit*, who invite guests to their homes, lull them with food and drink, and then bring them out to the yard to admire the zucchini. Old friendships begun in college years have felt their first chill because of withheld praise for a row of anemic rhubarb.

Fertilizer is a problem that has sundered neighborhoods. I have heard horse manure recommended as precisely the ticket for corn and Kentucky Wonder string beans. This opinion is regarded with contempt by the advocates of cow manure, who say that horse manure, for reasons known only to horses, is too acidic to be of any use.

They are both wrong. One of the imperishable bits of wisdom I retain from my heedless youth is the superiority of sheep manure. When young, I heard some of the wisest men I know (many of them with families) declare: "Put your sheep manure to your lawn in March when your spring rains can get at it."

One authority assured me that this also discourages lawn-crossers, who hesitate to tread the easy hypotenuse through grass spread with sheep dressing.

If you want the rest of my folk wisdom, it consists of two instructions: Take off your storm windows on April 19, and never buy raffle tickets from out of town.

There is no real defense against the newly converted gardener. I have seen a promising winter evening die like a sprayed aphid because the host wanted to go through Burpee's seed catalogue and to ask my opinion of whether he was ready for eggplant.

What I have done is to develop a phony interest in wildflowers in an attempt to fight boredom with boredom. The only wild flowers I recognize are buttercups, Queen Anne's Lace (sometimes called cowbane) and blue succory. But for conversational purposes I have developed an armory of flowers unknown to the Swedish botanist Linnaeus.

When my friends brag of robust beets, towering sweet corn and Hubbard squash as big as cauldrons, I counter with discoveries of flowers growing free for the gathering: flowering erysipelas, frugal hegemony, bat's breath, creeping pipefitter, common parsimony, shepherd's dowry, false cutpurse, medicinal hubris.

It may not be much of a defense, but it's all I have these summer evenings in Chestnut Hill.

WORDS NOT TO USE: A SUMMER SERMON

The following sermon was given on a recent Sunday at the Church of St. Barnabas the Less, Cobb's Landing, Cape Cod. It evoked considerable dissatisfaction.

The parish priest, Rev. Sylvester Feiffer, states that he had not expected Father Sweeney to ascend the pulpit, since Sweeney had always declined invitations to preach on the plea that he had no talent for it, a disclaimer that remains unchallenged.

We are grateful to Miss Maude Blunt of Boston, a summer visitor, for her shorthand notes. Since her conversion to Catholicism thirty years ago (an event referred to in some clerical circles as Cotton Mather's Revenge), Miss Blunt has devoted her energies to calling the attention of church authorities to what she calls the Iron Age of preaching. She has for most of this time forwarded to the Chancery transcripts of sermons she has heard. She has never received any thanks for this service, and in recent years no acknowledgements.

Dearly beloved:

Let me be brief and plain. Words not to use are "fantastic," "unbelievable," and "basically."

Do not use "hopefully" unless you make clear either that you are a cheerful person or that you expect a favorable result.

Accept the respectability of the objective case. "Between you and me" is good English.

"Irregardless" is a charming illiteracy which one can enjoy in public orators, but should not tolerate in the young.

Avoid "special" as you would strange drinks or the blue-plate lunch.

Don't use superlatives unless you are an expert and have canvassed all the alternatives.

Avoid using "so" as a discreet adverb. (Whenever I read "I thank you so very much" I fill out some handy apodosis like "....that I have broken out in hives.")

It is better to use "majority" to describe numbers, not parts of a unit. Otherwise you must accept: "I ate the majority of the lasagna, while my wife polished off the minority."

Don't say you have "come up with an idea" unless you do your thinking in the cellar.

Stop saying "You know" unless it has become an indispensable part of your speech rhythm. (Alas, I use it all the time, you know.)

Don't address people by their given names unless you know them well or are at a Rotary meeting.

Don't call the Supreme Court of the United States the "High Court," no matter where you may have read it.

Go to the wise man of the village and ask him to teach you to the difference between "lie" and "lay."

Don't say a custom is "More honored in the breach than the observance" unless you intend Shakespeare's meaning.

Boston Common is not Boston Commons; the Public Garden is not the Public Gardens; Boston is not the "Hub of the universe," but the Boston State House is "the Hub of the solar system."

Avoid sarcasm and the Celtic litotes.

"Literally" will scuttle the most seaworthy metaphor.

Think of the sentence, "Taking our seats, the curtain went up" — and avoid the dangling participle as you would a stopover in Philadelphia.

If a learned essayist uses the word "meaningful," stop reading at once.

The sermon notes end here. Her fears having been realized, Miss Blunt resumed her prayer book.

RED SHOES ON THE ANDREA DORIA

An old passport records my departure from New York on June 12th, 1956, and arrival at Naples on June 20th. It was almost the last voyage of the *Andrea Doria*. She made one more complete voyage from Genoa to New York and back; on the next westward sailing she went down off Nantucket on July 25th.

The embarkation was the usual headlong clamor in the vast pier shed, with porters pushing trucks piled high with baggage, passengers forming long lines at the passport control booths, then pouring up the gangways with a carnival crowd of visitors.

I must sort out this memory from many embarkations, at most of which I was the well-wisher rather than the seagoer. The one I remember best was the departure of a friend of mine for Rome. Part of the crowd were a few hundred (it seemed) Sisters in uniform who thronged the decks and public rooms, eddied through the dining saloons, spun the great teak and brass wheel in the wheelhouse.

When the all-ashore gong sounded, and the basso profundo ship's horn shook the decks, the Sisters trooped off and gathered on the pier—all but two. At the rail, Mother Superior and her secretary gave finger-tip farewells to their friends, who were waving handkerchiefs and calling out inaudible pleasantries.

On the promenade deck of the *Andrea Doria* five disconsolate musicians played "*Arrivederci Roma.*" Paper streamers spun out from the rails, and the little tugs gathered around the great liner like suckling puppies. Then the tugs left us and the engines quickened, mist gathered on the towers of New York, and we were alone with the ocean.

My next memory is the steady heartbeat of the ship and the whisper of the sea bringing on deep sleep. I would be up early to go over to First Class to offer Mass in the little baroque chapel.

The *Andrea Doria* is often called a luxury liner; well, in First Class it was, though not so much as the old *Queen Elizabeth* or the *France*. In the public rooms there were some excellent tapestries in cheerful green and blue, and some good modern Italian sculpture. A bust of Admiral Doria, the Genoese for whom the ship was named, stood on the landing of the staircase descending to the grand salone.

Cabin Class was rather cramped, with narrow companionways and staterooms reminiscent of a roomette on the Owl. I drew one of the two upper berths, which gave me a porthole occasionally subtended by a blue line of sea. My only concern was that in my early morning descents I might step on the elderly gentleman in the lower bunk.

My companions at meals were a composer from Virginia, a badly crippled man traveling to Bayreuth with his valet. The fourth person was a Florentine countess who ran a dress shop in Los Angeles. The conversation ranged from Wagner to the patchwork of Italian dialects and the rhetoric of Italian gestures. It was all so peaceful and civilized, the courtesy of people listening and replying. The ship was a floating township of peace and courtesy, with the sea listening and replying.

Time turned on slow wheels, twenty-three hour days eastward, twenty-five coming back. Reading and snoozing in a deck chair were serious occupations, or drinking bouillon or watching the dolphins cavorting in the bright sea like heraldry come alive. Forward on the boat deck we could hear the snap-snap of target rifles; shooting clay pigeons was a morning diversion.

At the harbor of Gibraltar, during the two-hour stop, the ship was surrounded by peddlers' boats laden with wicker baskets and straw hats, garish scarves and small rugs in ardent colors. The peddlers would hold up their wares and shout the price. They threw lines up over the rail and the money went down in baskets; then the peddlers would hoist up the souvenirs.

The Bay of Naples was too closely built down to the shore to be the dramatic scene I had expected. But later, viewed from Posilipo in the hills, the lovely sea gate curved like a shell. Off to the south, Vesuvius wore its panache of smoke.

Oh yes—in packing to disembark at Naples, I left behind a pair of red canvas shoes I had bought in Boston and now found superfluous, and surely out of place in Rome. I had worn them walking the morning and evening mile around the promenade deck. Perhaps they are still there in the drowned ship off Nantucket.

My selection as one of the speakers tonight alarmed me when it came and has brought me increasing panic since.

The invitation reminds me of another request I received two years ago. The Physics Club at my University asked me to address their annual Communion breakfast, and when I demurred, the young man who had called on me, wearing a slide rule in a sheath at his belt like a bayonet, said, "We tried to find the faculty member who was the furthest removed from science, and we thought of you." I declined though I expressed my gratitude for being selected as the spokesman for mankind before the invention of the wheel.

I hope that my name was not the premise for my selection. When Mr. Eliot first visited Boston College he remarked that the reason the name Sweeney occurs so often in his poetry is that there were people of that name whom he liked. I have always resisted the temptation to reply in the way that St. Teresa of Avila, in somewhat similar circumstances, is said to have replied to God.

Mr. Eliot's achievements have been so massive, the tide of his influence has thundered on so many beaches and brimmed so many harbors that the books explaining him must far exceed Dr. Eliot's five-foot shelf. He still abides the scholars' question, and the common reader finds new depths and fresh riches with each rereading.

It was not only that Eliot, as Ezra Pound said, had superbly prepared himself for the craft of poetry, but that he brought to his writing desk a schooled and tempered heart which gave its reserved but compassionate resonance to everything he wrote.

For a generation that found "old truths uncouth," which had been told often enough from the lyceum platform and the university rostrum that the past was an attic store-room of faded tintypes and broken clocks, he said this:

"Someone said: 'The dead writers are remote from us because we *know* so much more than they did.' Precisely, and they are that which we know."

He said more:

"No poet, no artist of any art, has his complete meaning alone. His significance, his appreciation is the appreciation of his relation to the dead poets and artists. You cannot value him alone; you must set him, for contrast and comparison, among the dead."

It was the sense of the past, the historical sense, which Eliot says made the writer at once traditional, and still most acutely in touch with his own time:

"The historical sense compels a man to write not merely with his own generation in his bones, but with a feeling that the whole of the literature of Europe from Homer and with it the whole literature of his own country has a simultaneous existence and a simultaneous order."

The word *order* is a useful one for a description of Mr. Eliot's work and of his life. At the end of his Theodore Spencer Lecture in 1950, he found the highest function of art,

". . . .in imposing a credible order upon ordinary reality, and thereby eliciting some perception of an order *in* reality, to bring us to a condition of serenity, stillness and reconcilation. . . ."

The same quest for order (which Louise Imogen Guiney had called the passion for perfection) led him to elaborate his ideas of what culture is, and to address the possibility of a Christian society. The latter lecture is most challenging not only because it is as conscientiously clear as the poetry is indirect, but because he relates religion closely to a fruitful national culture. So much so that he says that "we need to recover the sense of religious fear, so that it may be overcome by religious hope." And again: "If you will not have God (and He is a jealous God) you should pay your respects to Hitler and Stalin." And finally: "Good prose cannot be written by a people without conviction."

These ideas, enunciated twenty-fours years ago, he referred to again last year apropos of C. P. Snow's book, *The Two Cultures:*

"One reason why I could not interest myself in the recent discussion about Sir Charles Snow and Dr. Leavis is that I believe—and I wrote an essay which seems to make the point—that culture springs up with and in the practice of a religion: the major cultures have been in the past so closely involved with the major religions as to be the other aspect of the religion. Neither Sir Charles Snow nor Dr. Leavis appears to take that view."

This same commitment to an order in the world had its strongest and most astonishing epiphany in the poetry. He had shown us "fear in a handful of dust." Now he showed us faith and hope in a "crowned knot of fire." The end of the Fire Sermon, and the last words of the entire *Waste Land* foreshadow the turning and climbing of the poet's mind. From now on it was as if Mr. Eliot had come out on a headland with a great landscape unrolled beneath it. He spoke as a believer exulting in his belief: not that the bronze oracular trumpet was placed at the service of religion, but that the man who spoke was "a religious and learned poet," as Harvard, his Alma Mater, proclaimed him in giving him his honorary doctorate in 1947, in the same month that Princeton cited him as "the literary conscience of our era."

It is possible, but I think difficult, to exaggerate the effect of Mr. Eliot's Christianity upon the academic world. Here was a man who had gotten rid of all illusions, and then, still completely disillusioned, had come upon the Christian faith as something beyond illusion. He made the possibility of Christian faith a living issue again on the campus. And he did it at much personal cost. Recently Mr. Eliot has said:

"I observed many years ago that one advantage of living in a post-Christian age was that no one could say one had become a Christian for respectability's sake."

His affirmation of an order, a providence, a revelation, a presence, cost him many admirers. I have always thought that the

"Journey of the Magi" was fully as autobiographical as the *Quartets*, and that this simple poem, written for a Christmas card, had as much blood and sweat upon the page as has one of the Terrible Sonnets of Hopkins. Perhaps one day Mr. Eliot will explain the poem more fully to us, though he has refused to explicate the *Quartets*, saying that if he did he would say something else. Recently he observed: "I often find other people's poems very obscure but my own seem to me quite clear and simple."

We can say of him what Paul Valéry said of Bossuet: "He is a master of language, that is, of himself." And the order of his work is the impress of his ordered life, and the "serenity, stillness, and reconciliation" of his heart. Those whom he honors with the peerage of his friendship, see some of the playfulness which the reader catches only in the cat poems, and in his titling the great Christian play of this century as if it were a detective story.

Last year when a boy from Westminster School was granted an interview, the young journalist rang up Mr. Eliot a few weeks later, and with great excitement asked to see him again. Mr. Eliot consented, and the young man explained that there had been a deplorable misprint in the article, and the magazine was already coming from the press. The boy had asked, with respect to Prufrock, "Did the person you had in mind represent the age, or is he a character from *The Waste Land*?" As the question appeared in the school magazine, it read "Did the person you had in mind represent the age, or is he a character from *The Washstand*?" "Never mind," Eliot said to the crestfallen boy. "Remember that a misprint in a first edition makes it more valuable."

I remember, I remember. I remember the bustle of Eliot's arrival in Boston at the Back Bay Station, not far from the gymnasium where he had taken boxing lessons; not far from the Greek restaurant where he had sat at his ease with cronies like Conrad Aiken. I remember his gracious home in Kensington, and the gentle ribbing of Christopher Fry over some of his latest work in behalf of radio and cinema. I remember most of all a winter's night with the frosty heavens a drift of stars over Boston, when Father Joseph Appleyard and I were hosts to Christopher and

Valery Dawson and Tom and Valerie Eliot. It was in the dining room of the Ritz Carlton Hotel overlooking the Public Garden. Eliot and Dawson had not met for twenty years.

How widely the talk ranged over English folkways and English town names, brass rubbings and books and English cheese, bull fighting and the *taurobolium*, the New English Bible, the London theatre, and the staging of *Murder in the Cathedral*.

Serenity, stillness and recollection—and endless humility. They are Eliot's own and they are ours as we follow him through the fens and hedgerows of the poems, to "the gloomy hills of London, Hampstead and Clerkenwell, Campden and Putney, Highgate, Primrose and Ludgate"; and at last to the city beyond time.

Let us say, all of us gathered here in the heart of New York, let us say to Valerie and Tom Eliot that tonight our thoughts and affection are united in one outcry of gratitude to them, for whom truth has flowered in unfading beauty:

> When the tongues of flame are in-folded
> Into the crowned knot of fire
> and the fire and the rose are one.

The Campion Award Dinner
New York City
October 24, 1963

THE THANKS OF EZRA POUND

One day in the spring of 1958, Robert Frost, in his eighty-fourth year, left his grey Victorian house on Brewster Street in Cambridge and went down to Washington. At Back Bay Station in Boston his secretary, Kay Morrison, saw him aboard *The Senator*, which would bring him into the capital at supper time.

In his room at the Hotel Jefferson he worked through the night trying out his thoughts in the clear, rough script that was like a spill of stones across the page. Nothing came right until at dawn he knew what he wanted to say, and then he wrote "like lightning."

In the morning he walked into the office of Attorney General William P. Rogers and presented his petition for the release of Ezra Pound. He had been there before on the same errand, always with a committee. But the time had not been ripe, and perhaps the Attorney General had been wearied by the number of pleas in Pound's behalf. Like many others, Frost felt it a duty to continue the effort. "He did a lot for me," Frost said more than once. "I must never forget."

When Rogers had heard Frost out, he looked at the fresh-faced old man in a suit of grey with a touch of lichen in it. Then he spoke quietly, and the twelve-year struggle was ended. The Government of the United States would no longer oppose the motion for Pound's freedom. Frost should engage counsel to prepare the legal forms, and the Government would agree to the release.

The Washington law firm Frost approached did the work gratis, and the thousand-dollar check Ernest Hemingway had sent from Cuba to help with legal expenses was not needed. With Thurman

Arnold appearing for Pound in Federal District Court in Washington on April 18, Judge Bolitha J. Laws freed the prisoner in the care of his wife and guardian, Dorothy Shakespear Pound.

Later that year Frost told me of his part in the final successful move. Some time after the hearing he had received a bombastic letter from Ezra Pound, with no mention of thanks. It was a melancholy confirmation of the testimony Frost had given. "Pound," Robert Frost told me sadly, "is nuts."

There had been a cloud of eminent witnesses about Robert Frost when he met the Attorney General. Among those who had kept the cause alive were notably Archibald MacLeish in America and T. S. Eliot in England. There is a thick file of letters written by Eliot enlisting support for Pound.

When Eliot died on January 4, 1965, Pound cabled from Italy asking whether, if he came to the memorial service, he would be received. When Mrs. Eliot reassured him, he came to London and attended the service in Westminster Abbey. He sat impassively while the choir intoned the anthems in the language of the Authorized Version that Eliot loved, and while the voice of Sir Alec Guinness, all woodwinds and deep strings, made as pure a music with a reading from the *Quartets*. Then the muffled bells tolled along Thames' side for this good man, Tom Eliot of London, whose name would soon be graven on the Abbey pavement among the poets and the kings.

The day following the memorial service Pound came to Eliot's home in Kensington to express his sympathy to Valerie Eliot. In the hallway Eliot's big brown hat hung on its peg, and a handsome old umbrella stand sprouted his walking sticks.

Pound sat for a long time before the fire in an armchair—"Tom's chair"—in the lovely green living room. Mrs. Eliot waited in silence. Then Pound spoke, almost for the first time since his return to London: "He did much more for me than I ever did for him."

ROBERT FROST: HIS HUNDRETH YEAR

Once on a visit to Boston College, Robert Frost said: "If I live to be a hundred I'll be half as old as the Republic—and I'm just mean enough to do it, too."

Today is his hundredth birthday. He missed the century by eleven years when he died on January 29, 1963, at Peter Bent Brigham Hospital, believing to the end that he was going to recover. It was the same hope that had sustained him in other bitter times.

Recognition had come late. His first book was published when he was almost forty and living in England. With his four Pulitzer prizes and close to fifty honorary degrees, still year after year he waited for the Nobel Prize, as well he might have, for the gunpowder had blazed in Stockholm for Sinclair Lewis and Pearl Buck.

Family troubles lowered like carrion birds settling on his rooftree. There are emblems (a favorite word) of his suffering in "Home Burial," "Tree at My Window," "Acquainted With the Night," and many more.

Once he lectured at Rockhurst College in Kansas City. On his return he told me that he had stayed at the Jesuit residence, in the room reserved for visiting bishops. On the wall was "Christ writhing on the Cross." Here the president of a greeting card company had called on him with the request that he write verses for cards. Frost replied that there were other emotions than love.

It was in the serene last six years of his life that I knew him, reveling in his friendship, collecting memories that will see me through a happy old age like apples and crocks of honey in a keeping cellar.

"I have come to value my poetry almost less than the friendships it has brought me," Frost wrote to Louis Untermeyer. But what a hearth-light of friendship went out from him!

He came to Boston College in the spring of 1957 and read his poems to the first of the audiences that would gather in growing numbers for his six annual visits. "I am stirred," he said as the audience rose to meet him with a mixture of exuberance and awe. Then the storm of applause broke as he reached the platform.

He had a resonant voice, deep and musical, as he "said" his poems. Between the poems he would ruminate almost as if talking to himself, or teach the audience a lesson in prosody, lifting his forefinger to beat out the meter. Sometimes he joshed the critics, or scolded them. "Don't degrade the poem," he said to someone who had read an attraction for suicide into "Stopping By Woods on a Snowy Evening."

Once at the end of his reading the joyful audience surged around him and swept him out of the hall and down the steps. I feared that at eighty-five he would lose his footing or be crushed. When we had gotten him safely into the car a man near me said, "Can a little girl speak to Robert Frost?" Then he lifted the child and inserted her head into the car window.

"Mr. Frost," the child said, "I sent you a birthday card and you never answered."

With the lecture over, he could relax at a reception with student writers and a few faculty members and alumni. He was most at ease with college students, and would ask them to sit on the floor around his chair.

Once when we had brought him back to Brewster Street in Cambridge, when I said goodbye to him at his front steps I raised my hand over his noble head and said the words of the ancient Latin blessing. Then he turned and went into the darkened house.

Perhaps he recalled that when I saw him at the national birthday party in Washington, the spring before his death. That had been a triumphal day for him. Congress had voted him a gold medal. He had been at the White House for luncheon with President Kennedy. In the evening a great company of his friends gathered for a banquet at the Pan-American Union. In the lobby, where tropical plants surrounded a tinkling fountain hewn out of Mexican granite, I saw Justice Frankfurter, who was to give the address, the Ambassador of Great Britain, Robert Kennedy, James Reston, Theodore and Kay Morrison, a squirearchy of senators, poets and historians. Two young Ballantines, Frost's grandchildren, would turn up at a table with me along with Leverett and Alice Saltonstall.

The guests moved up the granite staircase of the Hall of the Nations. At the head of the stair, flanked by Stewart Udall and the president of Henry Holt, his publishers, Robert Frost gave us welcome.

He took my hand in both his hands and said, his blue eyes twinkling, "Now I am blessed." It was half joshing, half affectionate.

On his hundredth birthday I bless him still.

REMEMBERING AUDEN

When Wystan Hugh Auden quitted New York last year to live in Oxford he left an apartment that was cluttered with the baggage and sutlery of a long literary career. One of the perils of bachelor living, without wifely ultimatums, is the steady accumulation of debris that silts in and erases familiar landmarks. Yet the ruck is sometimes not as disorderly as it seems.

There is a kind of domesticated wildness about his poetry, a brook running underground, a gale caught to turn cornmills. Every experience was grist, yet his art often drove him (to abandon the metaphor) to a second milling.

Once when he came to Boston for a reading, I said, "You'll read 'Under Which Lyre,' won't you?"

"No, I won't," he said. "Sometimes you realize that a poem is a fraud." I protested that the poem rang true for his readers; but he would not read it.

When we were waiting in an anteroom while a crowd gathered in the gymnasium, I said, "The Boston audience either arrives early and reads a book, or comes in with a rush at the beginning of a lecture. Shall we begin at about three minutes after the hour.?"

"Certainly not," he said. "We'll begin at the announced time." And just at eight o'clock he picked up his books and walked out to the podium in Roberts Center.

He stood hunched over the lectern, a tall man in a rumpled dun suit and grey carpet slippers. He read without dramatic emphasis, his voice husky now but clear, letting the poems unroll their music like bolts of tweed and broadcloth. He did not ''speak'' his poems as Frost did, lifting his forefinger like a schoolmaster, nor rock his shoulders with the meter as Eliot did.

After one reading he said, "I hope there's no reception."

"Yes, there is," I said. We had had receptions on his four previous visits, and I had mentioned it in the correspondence.

"Well, a short one," he said. But he stayed on for an hour, answering questions courteously, his mind elsewhere.

When the mood was on him he seemed to enjoy the adulation and the questions of undergraduate poets. A girl asked him to sign a page in an anthology. He sat down and revised several of his poems, and handed the book back.

Once the wine ran out too soon, and I approached him where he stood in a group, an empty wineglass in his hand. "We've sent out for wine," I said. "It was improvident of me not to have gotten more."

"It was cheap," he said amiably.

One dinner before a reading is bright in my memory. One of the guests was Father Martin D'Arcy, who had been a young don when Wystan had come up to Christ Church. Auden was at his most brilliant and merriest. Around the table we reveled in the rich flow of reminiscence, at the evocation of the boats on the Isis, the running of the Christ Church beagles, the Oxford churchbells ringing their changes on Sunday mornings.

One personage Auden recalled bore the raffish title of "the second wickedest man in Oxford."

"Don't mention his name," said Auden, laughing at his own trace of superstition. "The last time I heard his name mentioned I lost my railroad ticket."

He was generosity itself. (Remember his going bail for Dorothy Day when she was jailed for refusing to participate in an air raid drill?) He came to Boston College for a minimum fee, even though lecture fees were an important part of his income, because his readings here began in his early years on the lecture circuit.

"Will you return to America?" I asked him last year. "Oh, yes," he said. "I'll have to come back."

The reading was planned for February 19, 1974. Perhaps because of the fear that this might be his last appearance in Boston, there had never been so much excitement at the prospect of his return. I worried that the hall might not hold the crowd of youngsters from all the universities in Boston who would come to listen and to say goodbye.

He was an original, humorous, patient, completely candid and radically humble man troubled by genius and by an emblematic intelligence. The apparent disorder of the apartment in St. Mark's Place was an emblem too: he knew where everything was. Along the coastlines and harbors of letters, in the present hour's constant labor, and in the life beyond time, Auden knew where things were.

ARNOLD TOYNBEE: THE PERFECT FRIEND

The train for York drew out of King's Cross station in London at 8 a.m., and would arrive at York well before eleven. Feeling virtuous at getting an early start, I sat down in the dining car, opened the *Daily Telegraph*, and ordered my breakfast. For 97 pence I had orange juice, toast, marmalade, and coffee. Around me some hearty eaters, in starched cuffs and pin-striped suits, were hoeing into the two-pound breakfast.

Under a grey sky the flat scenery of Bedfordshire and Cambridgeshire replaced the dingy bricks and green backyards of the London suburbs. As we neared the West Riding of Yorkshire there were yellow mown fields dipping down to the railroad line, with square bales of hay, and huddles of sheep, and white farm buildings.

York is a spic and span city of 100,000, once England's northern capital. It was a flourishing town in Roman Britain, garrisoned by the Sixth Legion, where some of the emperors had visited. Constantine was proclaimed emperor there in 306 A.D. Thereafter it was a center of medieval religion, and commerce, and rebellion. York remembers its history, and keeps its monuments well.

From the railroad station I walked across a high-stepping bridge over the River Ouse, and explored the ruins of St. Mary's Abbey. This was a Benedictine foundation, once a center of religious influence. Its abbot sat in the House of Lords. From fragments of wall and bits of pavement one can visualize the geometry of nave and apse and Lady chapel.

Over the clean streets and the chimney pots, rising over the city wall with its six gates, is the Gothic bulk of York Minster, the largest medieval cathedral in England. It is beautifully restored, with its perpendicular arches of grey stone and colored windows making a panorama of light to rival Chartres. Under the Minster the ruins of the Roman capitol have been excavated, as if the past had been peeled back, century by century.

Seeing the ancient places, the stones of the plundered Abbey, and the half-timbered houses in the Shambles, the remains of a Danish settlement and a Saxon kingdom, and of a nation divided between King and Parliament, I felt that I was prepared for the errand that had brought me to York. I had come to say goodbye to Arnold Toynbee.

When I had been in England before we had had some happy reunions, twice at lunch at the Athenaeum, the gentlemen's club near Trafalgar Square. Toynbee had walked over from his office at the Royal Institute for International Affairs in St. James's Square. He was a tall, white-haired figure in grey striped trousers and black jacket. There was a quality of kindness about him like a fragrance.

On one of these afternoons at the Athenaeum the dining room was full of gentlemen in grey cutaways and ladies in long flowered gowns. The Queen was giving a garden party at Buckingham Palace.

When I had seen him last, in 1972, Mrs. Toynbee had cooked Sunday dinner for the three of us in their book-lined apartment at 95 Oakwood Court, Kensington. Toynbee was recovering from a stroke, but was able to read three days a week in the British Museum. One noontime the Director of the Museum was surprised to find Toynbee carrying a tray in the cafeteria line. He prevailed on Toynbee to take lunch in the Director's office, a concession Arnold accepted with reluctance.

Two years ago he had wanted to be nearer his children, and had moved to Yorkshire where his son, Laurence Toynbee, a painter, had built a house for his father. He and Veronica settled happily in Chapel Cottage at Ganthorpe, near Terrington, sixteen miles from York. It was familiar ground. In the attic of the big rambling brick house next door Arnold had written much of his *Study of History*. They lived in Chapel Cottage hardly two months.

Mrs. Toynbee had written me about the second illness, which had begun in August, 1974. Arnold was in a nursing home, with his left side paralyzed. His speech was largely unintelligible, but he was reading and trying to write. If I came I would be allowed to see him. Laurence Toynbee added his request that I visit his father and Mrs. Toynbee. "He may not know you," Laurence said, "but it will mean a lot to her."

Purey Cust Nursing Home is a large Georgian building set in a garden opposite York Minster. On the second floor, Mrs. Toynbee brought me into Arnold's room, where he sat in white pajamas and a blue bathrobe.

"He knows you," Mrs. Toynbee said. "This morning when I told him you were coming he said quite distinctly, 'Boston.'"

I stayed twenty minutes chatting with him, recalling his two visits to Boston College. He had come to deliver the Tobin Lecture in International Affairs, and a second time to lecture in the Humanities Series. On his first visit, Weston Jenks and I had taken the Toynbees to St. Joseph's Abbey in Spencer. It was the first time the Toynbees had seen a Trappist Abbey, although Arnold had close ties with the Benedictines, and had sent one of his sons to Ampleforth, the Benedictine school in Yorkshire.

His second visit was in mid-winter, when Boston was digging out of a blizzard. But the Toynbees were veteran travelers, and we trudged happily around Boston in the snow drifts. They saw the exhibits in the archives under the State House, and King's Chapel, and from the top of the Prudential Building we could trace how the seventeenth century town had been "wharfed-out" to twice its original size. At the Boston Athenaeum they were shown some of the treasures—Washington's library, the Stuart portraits, and the book bound in the skin of the author (a fad that never caught on).

I recalled some of these memories in a rather one-sided conversation, trying not to let him become disappointed because I couldn't understand his replies.

A nurse brought in his lunch, and Mrs. Toynbee and I went out for our meal to a restaurant a few doors from the nursing home. She told me of some of the events of the previous year.

His old school, Winchester, had invited him to visit for an honor reserved for its most distinguished alumni: prime ministers and viceroys and archbishops. This was the *Ad Portas* ceremony. The entire school gathered at the gate and the "head boy" delivered a Latin address of welcome.

Toynbee had composed a response in Latin, and delivered it from memory in the gateway of the school where he had learned his Latin and Greek sixty years before.

Then he had been a guest at Oxford for a few days, visiting his old college, Balliol, seeing Broad Street and the High, and Carfax, and the boats on the river; hearing the lovely clamor of bells on Sunday morning, hearing for the last time the Oxford curfew at ten o'clock—the bell of Christ Church ringing its hundred times.

In his year at the nursing home he had been first brought out into the garden on fair days, and with the help of a physical therapist had tried to walk. He never made much progress. His attempts at writing produced only some unintelligible lines. His ability to read declined, though he still wanted books in his hands. He looked for the daily visits of the Anglican chaplain.

Through rainy mornings and sunny afternoons, Arnold Toynbee waited.

When Mrs. Toynbee and I returned I stayed only a few minutes because it was time for his afternoon rest. I tried to tell him of my gratitude for the times when we had "tired the sun with talking" in London and Boston, and for the royal gift of his friendship. Then I said, "I would like to pray with you, Arnold." Mrs. Toynbee nodded.

I said the blessing from the Book of Numbers, "The Lord bless thee, and keep thee; the Lord show his face to thee and have mercy on thee; and the Lord turn his countenance to thee, and give thee peace."

Then I recited the Latin blessing, and he spoke intelligibly for the first time: "Thank you, Father."

A FRIEND OF LOU GUINEY'S

Gathered with the packets of letters and files of periodicals and ranks of first editions that are the treasure of the Louise Imogen Guiney Memorial Room at Holy Cross are the offerings of her friends—pictures and reminiscences and souvenirs of Louise. One group of letters, written in a square, stub-point script on white paper as crisp as watered silk, bears the signature of Alice Brown; and the Cole etching of Louise, which is reproduced in Miss Brown's luminous book about her friend, was Alice's gracious gift to Holy Cross. It shows Louise in profile, the keen eyes intent, the face poised for listening. And for a portent and a prophecy, there is a crown of laurel in her hair.

Alice Brown's letters testify to the interest she had in the memorial room, which through the years has become a place of pilgrimage for friends of Lou Guiney and lovers of her poems. Miss Guiney herself began the collection with the gift of the remnant of her father's library with "my love to my father's Holy Cross." General Patrick Robert Guiney, "the good knight of Boston who was my father," had been a student at the struggling college in the 'fifties.

But the memorial room and the collection of manuscripts and memories that were gathered about Patrick Guiney's books were the work of Father Michael Earls, S.J. who was by way of being parish priest for a generation to Catholic literary America. What an immortal day it was when he brought Lou Guiney to Worcester (as later he was to bring Paul Claudel, Katherine Brégy and G.K. Chesterton) to make her an honorary doctor of her father's alma mater!

Trusting that the mention of Holy Cross and Father Earls

would be introduction enough, I wrote to Alice Brown late in 1947 and asked whether I might come to see Miss Guiney's last surviving girlhood friend.

The reply was in the familiar angular script:

Your kindly letter was long in reaching me, and so I seem the longer in answering. It is good to hear from a lover of the work of L. I. G. I wonder if she hears all these voices continuing her praise. I shall be very glad indeed to see you and talk about our beloved L. I. G., but not quite yet. You will hear from me short-ly offering you a date to come, and I say again that you are her friend.

A little later came another note:

Dear Reverend Sir:

Though I don't know how respectful I ought to be since we've never met. But on Thursday the 22nd I think my desk will show fewer mountain tops, and we can conjure L. I. G. to be with us, though unseen. And if you have to tell me you're *not* Reverend, she too would smile.

Come by 2:30, won't you, and stay as long as you can.

As I walked from Brimstone Corner across Boston Common and past the State House and over the crown of Beacon Hill, I canvassed what I knew of Alice Brown and her long, intimate association with Louise Imogen Guiney. A young New Hamp-shire schoolmarm in her twenties, with a flair for short story writing, she had come down to Boston in 1885 and joined the staff of *The Youth's Companion*. Louise and Alice were spiritual kin and whatever the occasion of their first meeting, they soon became close friends. It was Alice Brown who took Louise to England for the famous walking tour on which they rediscovered the grave of Henry Vaughan in Llansantffread. On their return they founded the Women's Rest Tour Association and its little magazine *Pilgrim's Scrip*, to encourage other women to take their vacations as they had, with pack and stick, in foreign lands.

In 1887 Louise wrote of "my Alice": "She writes much and

prints one-third....She is truly, first, last, and all through, a votary of Literature, an artist, a severe lover and server of the best, with no reference at all to the problem of how to slice the bread and butter it."

But for all that, Alice Brown's rewards were always more generous than Louise's, who had to support herself by selling money orders and stamps as postmistress at Auburndale, and as a cataloguer at the Boston Public Library, before her first departure for England in 1901. Alice was a regionalist, as were Sarah Orne Jewett and Margaret Deland, who painted her pictures in the subdued green and silver and slate blue of New England local color. But her talent swung in a wide arc: short stories, novels, biographies; thirty-five books in all. And somewhere along the way one of her plays won a ten thousand dollar prize offered by a Back Bay Maecenas.

Pinckney Street slopes steeply down in back of the sprawling State House, a narrow cleft between brick houses that savor more of London than of Boston. Alice Brown sat in an armchair by the window of her dim second-floor sitting room; a white-haired lady, smooth-faced and deaf, and with a voice as clear as a little bronze bell. She was eager to talk of her beloved Louise, and I regretted that my pen could not keep up with the wise and witty flow of her voice. As it was, sometimes she said, "Of course, this must never be put in print,"—and I reluctantly closed my notebook while she recalled some story about Lou's family or literary Boston in the 'eighties.

All her letters from Louise she had destroyed because "She wrote things to me that she would not have written to anyone else." So she had sat in front of her fireplace and watched as page after page blackened and curled and broke into ashes.

Alice Brown's characterizations of her contemporaries were sometimes sharply candid. I asked her about a Bostonian *grande dame* (let us call her Mrs. Aaron North) who had held "literary evenings," where promising writers were invited to meet the reigning families and drink claret-cup and listen while a starveling 'cellist sawed Liszt in two, like the lady in the side-show. "Mrs.

Aaron North," said Alice Brown, "knew no more about literature than the cat's grandmother."

She was appalled at the evil of the modern world, its easy tolerance of injustice, and the vast patterns of cruelty which have drained the epithet "medieval" of all its pejorative force. It was a simpler, kindlier era sixty years ago when she and Lou Guiney sailed for Europe. And her voice rose with emotion as she spoke of those Arcadian days when they had explored together the fields and the dear ancient towns of England.

"She was so far above me!" she exclaimed. "There were deeps in her that no one could sound." On their walking tour Louise was always careful to attend Mass on Sunday, she recalled. Though she never attempted to win Alice over from her amorphous Unitarianism, once Lou said to her, "For you, it is as if the last fifteen hundred years never existed."

"What could she have meant by that?" Alice wondered. "Perhaps," I suggested, "Miss Guiney meant that people come to a deep love of the Catholic Church through different gateways. Miss Guiney's was the gateway of history." And as the shadows lengthened on Pinckney Street I spoke of the ancient faith by which Lou Guiney had lived. But the journey to faith is a long one, and all Alice Brown's journeys were over.

Before I left, Miss Brown asked me to fetch the wine and the biscuits from the sideboard and as I filled her glass with a port of character and honor she proposed a toast. It was to her own death and her homecoming in heaven. So much courage and hope were in the words, that I raised my glass with a prayer for the uncovenanted mercies. It was indeed, in Lou Guiney's phrase, a toast to be drunk standing.

That was seven weeks before her death. My last message from Alice Brown was the charming greeting she sent me for my ordination:

To Francis Sweeney, S.J.

Prayer and Blessings for his onward way. A whisper and many thoughts from Alice Brown.

It is dated June 19, 1948. Two days later, in her ninety-first year, she died in Phillips House, Massachusetts General Hospital.

BY POST TO E.B. WHITE

If I try to imitate anyone in my writing it is E.B. White. When I get to my desk after breakfast each day, I take one of Mr. White's collections of essays from the shelf and read for a half-hour.

Today I read a piece called "The Summer Catarrh" from White's book *One Man's Meat*. White had been reading a paper called "Daniel Webster and the Hay Fever" by Creighton Barker, which had appeared in *The Yale Journal of Biology and Medicine* for May, 1937.

On August 19, 1851, Webster wrote to President Millard Fillmore: "I have never had confidence that I should be able to avert entirely the attack of catarrh, but I believe that at least I shall gain so much in general health and strength as to enable me in some measure to resist its influence and mitigate its evils. Four days hence is the time for its customary approach."

Shortly afterward Webster wrote to Fillmore: "I go to Boston to-day where Mrs. Webster is and thence immediately to Marshfield. By the process thus far, I have lost flesh, and am not a little reduced. Yesterday and Sunday were exceedingly hot, bright days...The heat affected my eyes in the catarrhal fashion."

The letters touched a chord in me. As a hypochondriac of long forebodings, in rude health but expecting the worst, I can understand Webster down to the bone. One needs a friend who will listen with appropriate alarm to the recital of symptoms and glum expectancies. How appropriate for a man of Webster's stature that the President should be his confidant!

An experience I had this summer threw light on Webster's resistance to disease. I had been invited to an outdoor poetry reading in City Hall Plaza at noon. Rain was falling when I arrived; the poets and their audience, a scant thirty of us, were directed to an art gallery on an upper floor of City Hall. The reading went on for an hour and a half, and then I bolted to the Union Oyster House nearby.

At the oyster bar on the ground floor, I ordered a bowl of clam chowder, and as I waited I reflected on the history of this genial building. Like the Cheshire Cheese in London where Dr. Johnson sometimes took his meals, or Davy Byrne's "moral pub" in Duke Street, Dublin, which James Joyce frequented, the Union Oyster House is one of those places where robust memory waits on appetite.

There has been a restaurant here only since 1826. Before that it was a dry goods store selling silks and broadcloth from the cargoes of ships that docked nearby. Here Ebenezer Hancock, the first paymaster of the Continental Army, had his counting house. Between these brick walls from 1771 until April, 1775 thumped the printing press of *The Massachusetts Spy*. Somewhere upstairs Louis-Philippe taught Parisian French before going home to take the crown of a diminished monarchy.

Over the bar is an oblong wooden plaque lettered in gold on black, which reads:

The original U-shaped mahogany oyster bar where Daniel Webster was a constant customer. He drank a tall tumbler of brandy and water with each half-dozen oysters and seldom had less than six plates.

As I diffed into the steaming chowder, I fell into conversation with the small man, his bald head dark from many ancient sunburns, who was tending bar.

"Has Mr. Webster been in lately?" I asked.

"No, he hasn't," the man said, not looking up from his work. "He's dead." He added after a moment: "You should know that."

"It must have been all those oysters that killed him," I said. "That or the brandy."

"It was the brandy," the man said. "He was a drunk."

115

This was a harsh judgment on Webster, though indeed he was known as a serious drinker.

I thought the incident might bear repeating to E.B. White. I had written to him several times, either to comment on one of his essays or to invite him to lecture in Boston; and once to ask whether I might visit him at his farm high up on the crumpled Maine coast.

On my proposal for a visit, he replied that he had made the choice between writing and company. The invitation for a lecture drew a courteous refusal. White said he had no talent for lecturing. In a few days I had a letter from his wife Katherine saying that perhaps her husband hadn't had time to reply to my letter. (I had invited both of them, and had offered lodging at the Ritz Carlton, a hotel I knew they liked). Public speaking took so much out of him, Mrs. White said, that he had given it up long ago. Once he had spoken at a war-bond rally and it took him two weeks to recover. She had crossed out "two" and written "four."

My desire to meet E.B. White grew on the fact that I had known several other writers and had never met them. Thomas Merton corresponded with me for some years, beginning when he was studying theology at Gethsemane Abbey and I at Weston College. When *Seven Storey Mountain* was published, he gathered up the manuscript, part ribbon copy, part carbons, with many pages corrected in Merton's hand, and sent it to me.

Frank Sullivan, the humorist and monitor of clichés, had told me that I might visit him in Saratoga after he recovered from a bout of surgery. The summons never came. Flannery O'Connor had said that she would come to Boston to lecture and had reminded me of her difficulty in walking and that we must provide for that. Her last letter asked for prayers. The lupus that had disabled her was gaining ground.

Jack Kerouac wrote a few antic letters and knew of my admiration for the stream of lyricism that ran through his unweeded writing. (Alas, it diminished to a trickle in his last books). Once in a rambling telephone call he asked me to officiate at his wedding. His fiancée was Greek Orthodox; he planned to have a Greek ceremony and then one at his home church of St. Louis de France in Lowell. The plans for the Lowell ceremony never matured.

I am reconciled to the fact that I shall not see E.B. White this side of Jordan—and not because he will predecease me. (In 1955, in a letter to Robert W. Patterson Jr., White wrote: "I was born in 1899 and expect to live forever, searching for beauty and raising hell in general.")

Who could begrudge his insistence on being left alone with the farm chores and the typewriter? Tomorrow morning I shall reread his essay "The Ring of Time," his best, I think. Not then, but later, when the dusk is coming in over the Atlantic like a soundless tide, I'll drink a toast, in something less potent than Webster's brandy and water, to the good grey Vergil of our times writing his ecloges on a salt-water farm in Maine.

ALL THE DIFFERENCE

I opened my eyes on the cheerful green walls of a room on the third floor of the main building of Children's Hospital. It was a golden autumn day. The sunlight which came in the tall windows in oblique torrents seemed to be thin gold washing everything in the room. Outside my window the few leaves I could see were yellow and metallic like the golden bough of the *Aeneid*. An angle of Vanderbilt Hall, the Harvard Medical School dorm across Longwood Avenue, seemed golden too, as the opulent sunlight touched it.

It was a time of great calm and healing peace. Not even a passing ambulance, its bleat like an amplified heartbeat, disturbed the morning. For two days I had not been able to see very well, but now my eyes could focus; I could see the children's cut-outs on the wall clearly now—Donald Duck and a dancing elephant. I could see a nurse standing at the foot of my bed. I had a question for her.

"Was I operated on for coarctation of the aorta?"

"Yes," she said, "you were."

"Was it successful?"

"It was."

Then I knew why this morning, the first of fully restored consciousness after the operation two days before, had such a quality of poured-out sunlight and a joy that was charged with music.

> Two roads diverged in a yellow wood,
> And sorry I could not travel both
> And be one traveler, long I stood
> And looked down one as far as I could

To where it bent in the undergrowth....

My first understanding that I had heart disease came when I was six, when old Dr. George F. Curley unhooked the stethoscope from his ears and said angrily, "Another one of those hearts!" I was the youngest of six children; two sisters had heart murmurs—mitral regurgitation—and that was my diagnosis too.

My activity was necessarily limited thereafter, but not radically. I could not play contact sports, or games which required bursts of speed like baseball or track. But I liked bowling and horseback riding, and though I could not swim very well, some of my happiest summer hours were spent idling in the water or falling out of boats at Falmouth on Cape Cod or at Lake Nipmuc near my home.

I lost a year out of high school because of high blood pressure. At the beginning of my ninth grade my family had moved to Newark, New Jersey. Because of persistant headaches I was directed by a doctor to leave school and rest for a while. He brought me into a hospital for a week's observation, and then had me on a meatless diet for a time.

I returned to school, a year behind my classmates, and moving back to Massachusetts continued through high school. In college, during the spring of my sophomore year at Holy Cross, nosebleeds and headaches again brought me to a doctor who sent me home with high blood pressure. When I returned in September, the pressure was still high, and the college doctor advised me to give up college for the present and return home.

When I arrived home, my family doctor sensibly thought that I should have continued on at college under whatever limitations my condition would impose, but the decision had been made. I spent much of my time in bed, reading compulsively; I was fearful and depressed, getting more nervous and despondent as the days went by, well on my way to becoming a professional sick man.

Among the incalculable debts I owe to my Mother, I think most of this trying time. Ten years before, my Father had died of Bright's disease; a few years since an older sister had died of a heart complication. My Mother must have dreaded losing another child, but her sweetness and serenity never failed. She never showed the slightest annoyance or disappointment when I was in my most savage moods. Once when I was at table alone with her, despondent and almost in despair, I said, "Aren't you afraid I might take this knife and kill you?"

"No," she said quietly, "I don't fear that at all."

My family doctor believed that my condition was very likely caused by premature hardening of the arteries, but readily agreed to further tests. Early in December my Mother and I took the Boston and Albany train into Boston, and she left me at the Massachusetts General Hospital.

I was at Mass. General for about a week, and the doctors were about to discharge me with a confirmed diagnosis of necessary hypertension. Then one night a young Harvard Medical student, Bernet Maduro Davis, came to my bedside in the long ward where there were about thirty other patients. I knew him because he was the one who had written my history, and had explored me from scalp to toes like a historian pacing off a battlefield. He had been one of a group of students who had accompanied a professor on morning rounds the day before, when the professor had looked at me and remarked, "Perhaps a touch of Bright's."

At any rate, when the med student came to me that evening he brought a blood pressure instrument unlike the grey cuff and rubber bulb I was familiar with. It was a larger cuff, and the indicator was a large brass-bound dial like a ship's chronometer. He said he had borrowed it from Dr. Paul Dudley White. He took the pressure in both thighs, and the pulse in the femoral artery, and then said, "As a favor to me, do not tell anyone that I took the pressure in your legs. I'm going to write this up now."

The next day I was surprised at the number of doctors who came to examine me. The med student's diagnosis of coarctation of the aorta, a narrow place in the large artery leading from the heart, was confirmed by a diminished pressure in the legs, and, by x-rays, the characteristic notched ribs. I was taken into a small amphitheater for Grand Rounds, and exhibited, with a resident explaining my case on the blackboard. In answer to a question he hesitantly said that my blood pressure was 180.

I was advised to return to college the following year, to live a normal life, to avoid strenuous sports, to get a rest in midday if I could, but not to be too finicky about climbing stairs. I was not told of the prospect of probable death by my early thirties.

In September I returned for my junior year in college, and this proved to be the happiest year of my life, with some success in the college magazine, and a growing wealth of friendships. In my final year I played the campus literary man, got indifferent marks but some intramural prestige. I sold some poems, and wrote campus news for *The New York Times*.

In my senior year I made the decision to apply for the Jesuits. Surprisingly enough, they admitted me. I entered the Jesuits at Shadowbrook in Lenox on September 7, 1939. For two years I was cut off from the world in a way that is hard to describe. I read no newspapers or magazines, I never listened to the radio except once on the four-hundredth anniversary of the founding of the Jesuits, in 1940. I forgot what money looked like, and whose face was on the quarters and nickels. I had to give up my watch.

The novices, all fifty of us, slept in a large dormitory which had been the spacious attic of the old Carnegie mansion. The windows were open to all the whims of Berkshire weather. Sometimes there would be snow on the beds in the morning, but there was a supply of husky blankets. I used nine, but this was far from the record number. One novice used fourteen, arranging them below the mattress as well as above, because the cold sometimes came through the mattresses.

It was an idyllic existence, with much hard work, intense prayer, physical discomfort, wide reading in spiritual doctrine and lives of saints, some study in Greek and Latin and French. I was unable to tackle the harder jobs like waxing floors, chopping down trees, or washing heavy pots in the scullery. But I could scour toilets and wait on table and weed the vegetable garden. This for two years. The third year at Shadowbrook was somewhat the same, but with less physical work and more Latin and Greek.

It was an exciting year, and a permanently rewarding experience to go afoot through all this magnificence, and to find one's own literature among the columns and architraves of the classics.

Two years of philosophy followed, at Weston College, a Jesuit seminary near Boston. During this time an irregular heartbeat sent me to Dr. Samuel A. Levine, who prescribed digitalis for an arrythmia. And he brought up the possibility of heart surgery.

Between philosophical studies and theology, Jesuits either teach in a secondary school or do graduate studies. I was assigned to teach Latin and English at Cranwell School in Lenox. It was a happy homecoming to the Ethan Frome landscape. Things went along well until the spring, when I developed a low-grade infection, probably caused by a tooth extraction. Two periods of rest and treatment with sulfa drugs in a local hospital were unsuccessful, and so I was sent to St. Vincent Hospital in Worcester under the care of its Fallon Clinic.

Here my illness was diagnosed as subacute bacterial endarteritis. I was now quite thin and weak, and irritable as a brown bear. Dr. James T. Brosnan prescribed a continuous penicillin drip through a needle in my arm. This went on for twenty days, a million units a day. When my friend, Dr. Sam Levine, visited me, he assured me that I was going to recover, and when he examined the penicillin procedure, he said, "If I had you at Peter Bent Brigham I would not do anything different from what is being done here."

On my recovery, I visited Dr. Levine at his office in Boston. After the sticky electrodes on my chest and wrists and ankles had taken my heart rhythm, and the fluoroscope had moved up and down my torso, and the blood pressure gauge had flickered its pointer like a snake's tongue, I put on my shirt and sat down in front of the desk.

Dr. Levine, his fox face intent, lifted papers by their corners and read them. Then he raised his head and spoke in his clipped, musical accent.

"The endarteritis is cleared up—that's past tense. But in addition to the coarctation you have an aneurysm, a swelling in the aorta...you may die at any time."

Fear rose in my belly like a geyser. Dr. Levine continued. "We are working on something that may be ready for you before too long. If it's successful, you'll live forever. The rest of you is all well."

What should I do now, I asked. Continue, he said. Should I give up or postpone my theological studies? No, he said; never give up, "or they'll shelve you."

I returned to Weston College to begin study in theology, being given all possible exemptions and favors by my superiors. I fear that I took advantage of the situation and dramatized my condition. This Camille-like attitude I admit now as childish weakness which only accentuates the charity of my brethren, who must have known that besides being a sick man I was also a fool.

There was a good deal of pain at this time in the chest and the small of the back. At night I would be awakened by my heart beating rapidly, and I would pray for a while and then sit up in bed and read the poets I liked—Housman and Chesterton and Merton and Frost:

> The woods are lovely, dark and deep.
> But I have promises to keep,
> And miles to go before I sleep,
> And miles to go before I sleep.

Dr. Levine reassured me—the heart symptoms were due to indigestion or nerves. The house doctor, Dr. Robert York of Watertown, was my great support during these four years of waiting. Now and then he would clip out of the *Journal of the American Medical Association* a report on the progress of heart surgery. His confidence and optimism prepared me for what I knew was now inevitable.

I was helped at this time by a passage I read in one of the essays of Robert Louis Stevenson:

> It is best to begin your folio; even if the
> doctor does not give you a year, even if
> he hesitates about a month, make one

> brave push, see what can be finished in a
> week.....Life goes down with a better
> grace, foaming in full tide over the
> precipice, than miserably struggling to an
> end in sandy deltas....

My ordination to the priesthood came on June 19, 1948, and with renewed hope and joy that beggars all vocabularies I entered into the Temple. My first Mass in my home parish was a low Mass, because, being too careful with myself, I did not want to attempt to sing the solemn Mass. But I was able to say Mass later in parishes on Sundays during the fourth year of my theological studies.

The final year of the Jesuits' training is spent in a sort of postgraduate noviceship called tertianship. The thirty-day retreat, made first on entrance into the Order, is made again, there is intensive study in the Rules of the Jesuits, in the method of giving retreats and missions, and some practical experience in these activities, especially as chaplains in hospitals or military installations.

During the year Dr. Levine brought up again the matter of surgery. He had told me previously that Dr. Robert E. Gross had developed an operation in which the narrowed part of the aorta was cut out and the ends of the vessel drawn together. I was too old for this operation, which was being done then on children. But Dr. Levine, said, "We may have something for you before long." Now in the spring of 1950 he told me of the procedure by which a section of the aorta from a corpse was grafted into the vessel. He suggested that I make up my mind soon or forget about the matter. It was perilous, to be sure, but my situation was dangerous anyhow.

I saw Dr. Gross and was impressed by the cold, matter-of-fact, reserved manner of this man whose achievements are an entire chapter in the history of surgery in America. He suggested that I wait a while; he seemed not at all anxious to operate on me. But Dr. Levine had said now, or not at all. So I asked Dr. Gross to operate.

In late September I entered Children's Hospital in Boston, where Dr. Gross operated exclusively. I was kept waiting for a day because of the need for a suitable corpse, and actually three sections of aorta were available when the operation took place.

Now I was a supremely happy man. My Jesuit studies were completed. Two books I had been working on in my spare time were ready for the publisher. I assured my Mother, steadfast and calm as always, that this was what I had looked forward to, and that it meant deliverance.

Father Bill Donaghy, then President of Holy Cross, came to see me, and on the morning of the operation telegraphed, "Courage, faith, hope—up Galway!" From Gethsemani Abbey, Thomas Merton wrote promising his prayers. A message from Daniel Berrigan, my fellow Jesuit scholastic, told me that he would spend an hour in prayer in the chapel during the operation time. Father Michael P. Walsh, who had asked Dr. Gross's permission to be in the operating theater, said to me later, "No one can say that you don't have a heart; I saw it beating." From all over the Jesuit world, from my brothers who had humored and endured and sustained me with their kindness all these years there rolled in a great tide of affection and blessing.

Early on the morning of September 27, 1950, a Redemptorist priest came from the Mission Church to give me Holy Communion. Then I read the great Psalm of faith:

> The Lord is my shepherd, I shall not
> want...
> Yea, though I walk through the valley of
> the shadow of death, I will fear no evil:
> for thou art with me.

I closed the book, and the medication began.

At 8:30 I was taken into the green-walled operating room and turned on my right side under the great light. My left arm was strapped over my head. A cannula for blood transfusions was inserted above my right ankle. The incision was made from the back of my neck around the arm to the left nipple. Five ribs were broken and the left lung collapsed, and the delicate work of cutting into the tissues was done.

At the crucial moment the first assistant lifted the aorta between his fingers and Dr. Gross snipped the vessel and sewed in the ends of the graft—a continuous mattress suture, I believe. It was the twenty-sixth such graft he had done, and the longest section he had so far attempted.

In the amphitheater some of his students kept their eyes on their watches and noted the extraordinary length of time the aorta was clamped off. But Dr. Gross knew the capacity of the other vessels, enlarged by the burden they had been carrying. Once the blood pressure shot up, but was quieted; there was considerable loss of blood and eleven pints, donated by Boston College students, supplied the need.

At last the job was done, and the rib cage reconstructed with platinum wire and pins of bone. With a great wad of adhesive tape encasing my torso I was taken into the recovery room. It was about 5 p.m.

Dr. Gross removed his gloves and went immediately to the phone to call my Mother to reassure her. This act of courtesy, as much as all the achieve and mastery of his surgical genius, I remember with gratitude. I had asked my Mother not to come to the hospital that day, but late at night my brother was admitted to the recovery room, and half-awake and half-blind I saw my brother's face bent over me.

For a few days I lay immobile in the bright room, naked except for the sheet up to my middle and the carapace of adhesive; there was a blood pressure cuff on my arm, a drain in the wound in my left side; a tube draining my bladder into a jar at the side of the bed. I had to be cleaned and bathed like a child. The nurses who lifted me and spooned water and cracked ice into my mouth were half-shadows. Hearing came back first, and I remember the cheerful inanity of singing commercials from a radio down the corridor. With the blood circulating normally in my legs for the first time, my feet felt hot for some days. At the end of the week I was able to walk a few steps.

I had met some of the children in nearby rooms before the operation, and now their brief visits were a source of delight to me. One little girl of ten, a Dutch child from Curaçao, in a full skirt with horizontal stripes of green and white and red, was particularly close to me. Some days when the blood pressure was jumpy or the heart acting up, the nurse would not allow her to speak, but she would stand beside me looking at me, often when I would not know she was there. I do not remember her name, or what became of her, but the love that went out between us is still a precious and imperishable part of my life.

Four weeks after the operation I walked out of Children's Hospital, feeling light and new and put together right for the first time.

MORNINGS IN ROME

"What places do you remember best?" someone asked me.

It is hard to say. Thinking back, I feel like Jean de France, Duc de Berry, leafing through the glowing pages of his Book of Hours.

I remember flying north from Oslo, with the plane so close to the Rondane peaks that its silver skin seemed to scrape the dragon's back of the mountain range. And then at Tromsø the July sun came down to the horizon's rim and never touched it. I went to sleep in Arctic daylight.

One summer I spent a few days at Campion Hall, the Jesuit college at Oxford. One morning when I had gotten my toast and rashers from the warmer and had sat down at breakfast table, Ted Yarnold, the Master of Campion, said, "Professor Tolkien is in town. Ring him up at Merton. You might be able to see him."

"Is he in good health?" I asked.

"He seems to be. He came here for dinner a few weeks ago."

I had almost given up the dream of bringing Tolkien to America, and repeating the time when I had arranged for another writer's visa. I had gone down to the Federal Building in Boston and had sworn that T.S. Eliot, a "person of distinguished merit and ability," was my employee. And for two radiant days at Boston College, he was.

Merton College is only a tantalizing five minutes' walk from Campion Hall. I had often passed it as I walked through Christ Church Meadow.

Tolkien answered when I rang him up in mid-morning. He regretted that he could not allow me to visit him, and he recalled my several invitations to Boston.

"I'm sick," he said in a quick vigorous voice that was somehow ageless. "I've just come from the north of England and I'm packing to go to the south."

"If you are in Oxford when I return, may I come to see you?" I asked.

"Certainly," Tolkien said.

The conversation was almost finished. Could I tell him in a rush of words what he must already know?—That he had discovered and given to a new generation a kingdom of delight that had its own landmarks and townships and people and speech, a country as imperishable as Dickens' real London or Trollope's imagined Barsetshire.

"He doesn't need to lecture," Professor Leo Hines had said to me. "Just let him come to Boston and be crowned."

"Mr. Tolkien," I said, "you must know the respect and affection your thousands of readers in America have for you. Even though I can't visit you now, it is an honor for me to hear your voice."

There was a pause, and then Tolkien said, "That is the nicest thing you could say to me."

I remember a hot August day in Venice. The crowd was almost shoulder-to-shoulder in the Piazza, and the alleys leading to the little bridges were raucous with music from junk radios. It was Saturday afternoon. I attended a late afternoon Mass amid the bookleaf marble and faded gold of St. Mark's. Afterwards I noticed that a priest was hearing confession in an open confessional, and I recalled that it had been some time since I had been washed in the Blood of the Lamb. After I had made my confession in schoolbook Italian, and been counseled in pure Tuscan, and absolved in Latin, the priest asked, "Are you a Dominican?"

"No," I said, "I'm an American." It was a foolish question deserving a foolish answer.

The heat hit me again as I came out of the cool basilica. I decided to bow out of Venice and head north, even though I would be arriving at the University residence in Innsbruck a day earlier than I would be expected.

I got my luggage from the lovely hotel on the Grand Canal, paid my hotel bill with a deceptively large amount of lire, at the hotel's dock caught the *vaporetto* to the central station. There was a train leaving in an hour, and the ticket agent booked a *couchette* for me. A *couchette* is a shelf-like berth, one of six to a compartment, which, if you are not too fussy, is a splendid way to travel by night.

As we went north through Bolzano and the Brenner Pass, the breeze through the window turned cool. It was positively cold when the train left me in clean, silent Innsbruck. In the railroad station a few early-rising hikers were drinking coffee. I strolled through the empty streets awhile and inspected the River Inn, running a cloudy green, and the mountain looping up at the end of Maria Theresienstrasse, before lugging my suitcase down to the Sillgasse, my face fixed for breakfast. At that distance, and even though I had fled its heat and clamor, Venice seemed unreasonably dear.

But there were more luminous days in Rome. The rooms at 26 Piazza di Spagna, where John Keats lived, attract me as do the Lincoln places in Washington. I have spent hours in the apartment overlooking the Spanish Steps where Keats lived out his last days, attended by his faithful friend Joseph Severn. Once in the sitting room next to the room where Keats died I read the moving account in Walter Jackson Bate's biography:

> "Severn – I – lift me up – I am dying – I
> shall die easy – don't be frightened – be
> firm, and thank God it has come!"

I cannot count the times I have gone to the grave in the Protestant Cemetery where Joseph Severn buried him. The thin gravestone does not bear Keats' name, but the words he dictated: "Here lies one whose name was writ in water."

The lawn is well-tended and green around the grave, and the access walks are white stones raked each day. Once two American students came with me. On the way we stopped at a flower shop and brought an armful of white carnations to cover the grave.

The Protestant Cemetery is a Domesday Book of a culture that still drank from the Roman fountains. Germans, Swedes, Norwegians, English, Russians, Americans came to Rome to study *"le arti del desegno"*, or to visit the tombs of the Apostles, or to recover lost health. When Shelley was drowned off Viareggio his body was burned on the shore. Its dust is under a stone with the sea-change quotation from *The Tempest*.

Goethe's son is here, and a parcel of artists and scholars, like Franklin Simmons, sculptor, who was born in Webster, Maine, in 1837 and died in Rome in 1913. Adeline Belle Hawes, who was born at Bridgeton, Maine, in 1857, died at Rome in 1932. She had been professor of Latin at Wellesley College.

One of the more moving inscriptions is on a tomb supporting the recumbent figure of a young man in military uniform, carved in white marble. He is holding a book on his chest and there is a spaniel beside him. His mother may have written the inscription—I think she did:

> Amid these wrecks of earthly glory and cherished hope and where unfailing still "the dayspring from on high visits" reviving nature, is laid to rest the little that could die of Devereux Plantagenet Cockburn, late of the Royal Scots Greys, 2nd Dragoons, and first born son of Sir W.R.S. Cockburn Bart. N.S. of Far Off Britain, of deep and unpretending piety, of rare mental and corporeal endowments, he was beloved by all who knew him, and most precious to his parents and family, who had sought his health in many foreign climes. He departed this life in Rome on the 3rd of May 1850, aged 21 years.

Once on a visit to Rome I stayed at the College of St. Robert Bellarmine, a few Roman paces from the Pantheon. I visited the marvelous *Rotonda*, as the Romans call it, every day, and never tired walking its pavement and reading the inscriptions on the royal tombs that hem its perfect round.

I was there after the ceremony in St. Peter's Square at which Mother Elizabeth Seton was proclaimed saint; the City seemed full of happy American sisters that day. At the Pantheon, Gounod's "*Ave Maria*" issued every twenty minutes, as usual, from some hidden source. Was it a recording? I asked a guard. No, he said, there was an *organista*; he led me behind one of the altar-tombs where an old man in a rumpled grey uniform was at the organ keyboard.

I explained that this was an important day for Americans because of the canonization of our first native saint. Could he play "The Star Spangled Banner" or "America the Beautiful"?

"I could," he said, "if I had the notes." But he thought Americans would know "*Panis Angelicus*" and he played that with great spirit, and then threw in "Oh Holy Night." It may have sounded odd on a September morning.

The House of the Historians, next to the fortress-like Jesuit Curia on Borgo Santo Spirito, is only a shout away from St. Peter's Square. It houses not only a corps of writers but the staff of Vatican Radio, who broadcast news and religious programs in 28 languages.

I stayed with the Historians for a few weeks. Quite early I would walk down the Borgo and go around the clock dial of Bernini's colonnade to the door of St. Peter's. Workmen with twig brooms and garden hoses were cleaning the cobblestones. At seven o'clock the Swiss Guard were changing sentries at the door of the Basilica. They were not in their yellow and red uniforms but in the more serviceable horizon blue.

The sacristy is a separate building off the south transept. A young cleric with sparkling glasses, seated at a great desk, examined my identification papers and allowed me to offer Mass. I put on

the vestments while a small altar boy waited in purple cassock and white surplice. I was taking my time putting on the linen alb and heavy damask chasuble. The altar boy said quietly, *"Procedamus!"* Let's get going!

I took the dressed chalice in my left hand, with my right hand on top, and followed the boy down the marble corridor, through the transept, and into the nave. Bow to the tomb of St. Peter under the twisted bronze columns of the papal altar, turn to the right and genuflect to the Blessed Sacrament, and then the long walk between the cyclopean piers, under the architrave where the

scripture unrolled in letters as tall as a man: Thou art
Peter...confirm thy brethren...I shall give thee the keys of the
Kingdom of Heaven; past the immense statues of Francis and
Dominic and Benedict and Mother Cabrini and Loyola, to the
last altar on the left, just inside the bronze doors.

I seemed to be walking through time, as if history were a village
street that I was traversing from end to end. I was in tears when I
reached the altar I had chosen, and spread the linen and opened
the book, and bowed my head to the God who gave joy to my
youth.

And that was how, on a Roman morning, I said Mass looking
up at the *Pieta*.

A QUESTION OF CONFIDENCE

Father Colman Reynolds came out of a room on the fifth floor of Cushing Pavilion of St. Elizabeth's Hospital, and walked to the elevator. A middle-aged man in working clothes came from farther down the corridor and joined him in the elevator car. He inquired about the patient Father Reynolds had been visiting, and they agreed that the priest's mother and the middle-aged man's wife were getting excellent care.

"I hope my son is here," the man said. "He's going to pick me up at the door." But there was no sign of the son's car.

"Which way are you going?" the priest said.

"I'm heading for Cleveland Circle. I can get the street car there."

"Come along with me," Father Reynolds said. "I'm going through Cleveland Circle."

The man was a truck driver, he said. He had just brought a rig in from Detroit. You have quite a few strange experiences on the road. Just last week he had noticed a car by the side of the highway, and two women trying to cope with a flat tire. He had pulled the truck over in front of them, and gone back to help.

When he had finished changing the tire one of the women thanked him and left a bill in his hand when she shook hands. He put the bill in his pocket without looking at it.

Some miles down the road he stopped at a diner and when he took the bill out of his pocket he found that it was one hundred dollars. The two women had stopped at the diner. He approached their table and said, "I just noticed that the bill you gave me was a hundred dollars. Was that a mistake?"

"No," the woman said, "it wasn't a mistake. You stopped when we needed help. We can well afford it."

You often get chances to do favors for people. The truck driver had just gotten a television set for one of the nurses at the hospital for only twenty-five dollars. There had been a wreck on the highway involving a truckload of TV sets. Many of them were only slightly damaged but in the insurance settlement the truckmen's union was allowed to sell off all the sets for their benefit fund.

"Say, Father," the man said, "you've been very kind to me. Can I get you a TV set for twenty-five dollars?"

After some discussion the priest said "Yes," protesting at the low price. They agreed on five dollars more "for the dispatcher."

The man said that he lived in the sixteen-hundreds on Beacon Street; he would stop there and phone the union hall to see what sets were available. What was Father's preference?

He came out of the apartment building and got into the car, saying, "It's okay. They've got the set you want." He added sheepishly, "My daughter says I shouldn't charge a priest anything."

"No, no," Father Reynolds said, "you're doing enough for me as it is."

They drove downtown and stopped outside a loft-like building which the man identified as the union hall. He accepted thirty dollars and said, "I'll be out in five minutes."

Five minutes, ten minutes, a half-hour. "Incredible!" the priest said. "I've bought the Brooklyn Bridge!"

He got out of the car and when a police wagon came along he went out into the street and stopped it. "Go down to Station 2 and make a report," the police officer said.

At the station the lieutenant said, "That's what you get for buying stolen goods."

"I don't buy stolen goods," the priest said. "And if I did I wouldn't expect to meet the dealer on the fifth floor of St. Elizabeth's."

"It *was* a pretty good story," the lieutenant said, "one of the best I've heard. Well, there are four dives near where you left him. He might be in one of them. I'll ask two detectives to go along with you if you want to look for him."

The detectives were greeted jovially by the patrons in one of the barrooms, and there were numerous assurances that nothing illegal was going on in the place. One customer warned Father Reynolds that he was in bad company.

No sign of the missing man. Perhaps he was working another hospital, or changing tires for stranded ladies, or polishing up his act.

CROSSWALK

It was late afternoon on a grey November day, with the east wind bringing the smell of wharves and ocean into the Boston streets. I walked southward on Boston Common down the Long Path quartering the sloping fields between Beacon Street and Boylston. My mind wandered to the palimpsest the Common is. Here Ben Franklin tethered the family cow. Here the Boston schoolboys threw snowballs at the Redcoats. Here Boston hanged Mary Dyer, the Quakeress, and perhaps Mary Glover, convicted of witchcraft, who could answer the court only in Irish, and who had difficulty saying the Lord's Prayer. Down this Long Path Emerson walked with Whitman, while Concord tried to persuade Brooklyn not to publish *Leaves of Grass*.

Over on the concourse along Tremont Street, the Single-Taxers and the Born-Again Baptists, and the Hare-Krishna dancers were crying out to the unredeemed.

At the southern end of the Common a broken iron fence encloses a small graveyard where Appletons and Copleys lie under their thin slate gravestones. A young man came out of the graveyard, like one of the possessed men in Matthew's Gospel. He was dirty, not with the ingrained dirt of the city bum, but with the grime of sleeping out on the ground, and not having washed that day. He walked a bit unsteadily, and spoke too loudly, like a child bringing his playground voice indoors.

"Can I walk along with you, Father?"

As I said, "Yes, of course," a man some distance along the path turned and asked, "Is he bothering you?"

"No," I said. "I want to talk with him. But thanks."

The young man touched my sleeve for a moment with a soiled hand, and said, "I haven't eaten since yesterday morning. I was wondering...."

"There's a lunchroom near here," I said. "Let's go over there."

We walked down the mall where some of Boston's heroes gestured or meditated in bronze: William Ellery Channing, Charles Sumner, Wendell Phillips with his preposterous axiom graven on the pedestal: "Whether in chains or in laurels liberty knows nothing but victories."

The lunchroom was brightly lit and clean with its white and green tiles. As we took our places on stools at the counter, a tall, thick-shouldered waitress turned from the grill and saw him, the rumpled clothes, the grimy paws. "Oh, no," she said with a gesture, "not here!"

"Then I guess you don't serve me either," I said. We walked out, with not a word from him to save his pride.

"There's another lunchroom across the Square," I said, and we walked through the traffic past the statue of Lincoln with his hands outstretched to a kneeling slave. I was afraid of another rebuff, and asked him to wait outside. He stood on the curbstone, but looked in the window a few times to see whether I was still there.

The counterman grilled three wads of meat and wrapped the hamburgers in foil, and put them in a brown bag with a quart container of milk. Outside, we walked east and around the block. He quickly ate the hamburgers, and then talked on as he drank the milk in long gulps.

He had returned from Vietnam less than a year before, had landed a job, and things were going well. He lived in a city not far from Boston, say, Nashua, New Hampshire. He had come to Boston for a holiday three days before with a hundred dollars in his pocket and a brand new sports jacket. But one drink had merged into many and the money was gone, and, with great regret, the sports jacket. He had slept last night in the graveyard, where a few children had tried to rob him. He had jumped up and driven them off.

"Can I buy your bus ticket home?" I asked, pointing to the bus terminal in the Square. "You can be home tonight."

"No," he said, "I can't go home yet. And don't give me any money."

"Then what *can* I do for you?"

"Father, perhaps we should say some prayers." I agreed, and standing on the corner of Stuart and Carver Streets we said a too-loud Our Father and Hail Mary. "The Creed," he prompted, and so we said that while people stared from passing cars. Then he said, "Father, my parents are dead. We should say some prayers for them." So we did, with his tears coming now.

"Can I give you absolution?" I said impulsively. "Are you sorry for all the sins of your life?"

"Oh, yes, Father!" he shouted. And while he chanted the Act of Contrition I absolved him, and blessed his dignity and innocence. And so I left him.

I thought I might have heard from him in the months since, and I haven't. And yet I hear from him every day: when I awake in the night and grieve for my sins, for I trust God's mercy in the daylight, and fear His justice in the dark. I hear from him in the midst of my Mass and when I lift my head from reading Scripture, and try to understand the Word. Because he taught me, when I had almost forgotten it, what a priest is for: to feed the hungry, to give drink to the thirsty, to counsel the doubtful, to comfort the sorrowful, to forgive all sins, to pray for the living and the dead.

I would like to meet him again and thank him.